THE
PRIVATE
VAULT

THE
PRIVATE
VAULT

A Guide to Building Tax-Free Income
in the New Economy

Gregory J. Boots, JD

ANDERSON
FINANCIAL SERVICES, LLC

To Lori, my loving wife of 20 years, and to our remarkable sons, Tristan and Carson, as they carry the legacy to future generations.

DISCLAIMER

Contents

Introduction

The Private Vault

Are you in charge of your wealth or is your wealth in charge of you? Is it a source of empowerment or a source of worry? Too often in today's world, it feels as though our financial peace of mind is at the mercy of forces beyond our control.

Wild swings in the market have come to seem like the new normal. The real estate debacle has shaken what many of us used to see as the most reliable of assets. Upheaval in the financial and real estate markets in recent years has destroyed untold wealth and sowed deep insecurity throughout our society.

We certainly didn't need new sources of worry. It's tough enough to withstand taxes, inflation, and other forces that quietly work to erode our wealth.

All of these factors bring me to the purpose of this book. I want to suggest to you that it's time for a new and better approach to stewarding and growing your wealth. The method I'll lay out in the pages ahead is based on putting in place a structure that will deliver guaranteed returns on your capital, without putting it at risk, through boom and bust. This structure will provide you with the ability to access your capital at will, not when the government, your employer, or your bank permits you to. It will allow you to be in control of your wealth rather than being controlled by it.

Betting Our Future

What does it mean to lose money or make money in the market? Based on my years of experience working with clients, I believe most people fail to understand what's really going on. I've heard from a great many people recently that their investment portfolios are just now getting back to the levels they were more than a decade ago. Most of these folks credit this to market recovery—while ignoring the impact of the contributions they've continued to make year after year.

What if these investors had not had all of their funds at risk in the market? What if they had deployed their funds in an alternative strategy where market volatility wasn't a factor? The answer is that they would be in a much stronger position today. Even if the return on their investment was 0%, they would be far ahead simply because they would not have had to make up lost ground. It's a fundamental truth of investing that a negative return on an investment will have a much longer-lasting impact than a positive return.

What concerns me most is that, even as individuals voice relief over their portfolios being above water again, they could be setting themselves up for more pain. By remaining committed to their 401(k)s and investment portfolios that are exposed to market swings, they are putting 100% of their funds at risk. It's like being hit by a train, recovering from your injuries, and then continuing to walk along the railroad tracks.

The simple fact is that, while trying to achieve our long-term financial goals, most of us have put our wealth at great risk—and we only realize that fact when it's too late.

We invest our money in the retirement plans our employers provide us. We invest in the mutual funds companies offer us as packaged investment solutions. We shop for loans at our banks. As consumers, we use solutions that ultimately benefit the product providers far more than they benefit us.

Few of us understand that it's possible to be on the other side of the equation: Instead of consuming solutions provided by others, we can provide our own solutions. We can be our own bankers!

Becoming Your Own Lender

By becoming our own lenders, we create and enjoy access to what I call our "Private Vault": A resource that gives us true control of our financial resources and allows us to strategically build our wealth instead of depleting it as consumers.

Properly implemented, your Private Vault won't require you to change your lifestyle at all. But it *will* change the way you pay for things—allowing you, rather than finance companies, to benefit from your purchases. It will change the way you accumulate wealth by eliminating uncertainty and providing peace of mind. And it will put you on the road to controlling your own wealth and, ultimately, achieving financial independence.

As you'll learn, the means to create your Private Vault are custom-designed life insurance policies known as 7702 Contracts. See Appendix A. We'll also discuss how conventional financial wisdom, trumpeted by Wall Street and the banks, makes no mention of the potential that life insurance holds for achieving your financial goals. No surprise there—these institutions prefer to herd consumers into their go-to products, from certificates of deposit to mutual funds and IRAs.

If you want a testament to the power of life insurance, look at the people who use it as a key element of their financial strategy. Life insurance is a cornerstone asset used by a significant majority of the sophisticated, wealthy individuals whom I know and work with. These individuals use life insurance, typically either mutual whole life insurance or indexed universal life insurance, as the means to creating their own Private Vault.

Properly designed, life insurance policies help to free funds from the uncertainties of the market, from interest-hungry lenders, and from rules about when and how their owners can access their own wealth. But the benefits extend much further.

The same life insurance that's the foundation of the Private Vault provides tax-free income that can be used for retirement, college funding, or any purpose you choose. The cash value within these policies is easily accessible. The policies' death benefits pass free of probate and provide an additional means of providing for loved ones and paying estate taxes. Properly structured life insurance allows you to make greater charitable contributions with tax benefits; it can cover the legal and administrative costs of settling your estate, and it can even provide asset protection.

The Private Vault—your personal bank—can be the simple and powerful tool at the center of your lifelong financial strategy. This tool can stand alone as your main financial strategy, or it can be combined with other investment vehicles within a multi-faceted approach. As you'll learn, having a Private Vault through strategic use of life insurance can be an invaluable resource for families and businesses alike.

1

Where We Are
versus
Where We Want to Be

For millions of Americans, the prospect of a comfortable retirement used to be a foregone conclusion. We knew that around age 65 we could punch out of the workforce and count on our company pension, along with Social Security, to pay our bills for the rest of our lives.

But in just a few short decades, comfortable retirement has stopped being a sure thing. For millions of Americans, the subject of retirement has become a source of distress and apprehension. Today, the system that was the bedrock of retirement planning for generations has been smashed.

It's been replaced by a worrisome landscape in which the Social Security system is teetering, and in which individuals are somehow supposed to use retirement "savings" accounts such as 401(k)s to be their own pension managers.

Because those 401(k) accounts are the only kind of retirement solution that the past couple of generations have ever known, it's easy to forget what a radical change they represent. In fact, while most people think of IRAs and 401(k)s as their primary retirement vehicles, they were never intended to fill that role at all.

The 401(k) was developed from an obscure section of the Internal Revenue Code that was created in 1978. At first, 401(k)s were adopted as a way for workers to supplement their retirement income. Unfortunately, employers increasingly seized on them as a replacement for their company pension plans, and now most employers offer "defined contribution" plans such as 401(k)s and 403(b)s.

Such plans allowed employers to shift responsibility for retirement savings onto their employees. Basically, we all became our own pension managers without being told what was happening. How has this change worked out for employees? The results so far indicate a disaster in the making. The first workers to spend their careers in the 401(k) era are now approaching retirement age and they're nowhere near being ready.

As of 2010, the median household 401(k) and/or IRA balance for employees between age 55 and 64 was just $120,000. Many of us will live for 20 to 30 years after retirement. Could you and your partner live on $12,000 a year or less, even before inflation?

Individual Retirement Accounts (IRAs), meanwhile, were introduced in 1974 under the Employee Retirement Income Security Act. Like 401(k)s, IRAs were originally intended to supplement, not replace, pensions. There are now $270 billion in IRA assets. How do our defined-contribution plans such as 401(k)s, 403(b)s, and the like stack up? Their assets were $4.5 trillion at the end of 2011.

Corporate pensions are fast disappearing. From 1980 through 2008, the proportion of private-sector workers participating in traditional pension plans fell from 38% to 20%, according to federal government data.

Even government pension plans are in trouble. Nearly every state has made painful cuts to its pension benefits for public employees in the past few years. But these pension plans combined still face a gap of $800 million between incoming revenues and what they owe in retirement benefits, according to *The Wall Street Journal*.

The country's military pension system is in alarming shape as well. The Pentagon currently owes nearly $1.3 trillion more than it has, and this is expected to more than double by 2034.

The Erosion of Social Security

Americans are used to thinking about retirement funding as a three legged stool, with Social Security being one leg. Social Security was never expected to be as important as it has become. With the current Social Security crisis, the leg has become broken and we are left perilously balancing on that stool.

Social Security started out as being very limited in scope. Created in 1935 as part of Franklin D. Roosevelt's New Deal, it was only designed to provide full benefits at age 65, during a time when the combined life expectancy for Caucasians was 61.7 years and the combined life expectancy of African Americans was 53.1 years. In other words, Social Security was a kind of insurance for people who lived to be "exceptionally" old. The government knew most people would die before becoming eligible.

Today that equation has been flipped on its head. According to the United States Census Bureau, our combined life expectancy for 2015—regardless of race—is going to be 78.9 years. It's no wonder the system is on the road to insolvency.

In any event, many Americans have an unrealistic reliance on Social Security in their retirement planning. The system is designed to replace just 40% of an average wage earner's income, yet most financial advisors say retirees will need 70% or more of preretirement earnings to live comfortably. Social Security was designed to be a supplement—not a replacement—for other retirement-income sources.

If projections stay on course, Social Security benefits will soon have to decline sharply. The reason is simple: More money is going out of the system than is going in. By 2033, incoming revenues and revenues from the Social Security trust fund will no longer cover the costs of full benefits. As a result, the government would have to slash full benefits by at least 25%. This reduction is needed to fix the current $8.6 trillion shortfall in promised benefits.

Many Americans assume that full Social Security benefits will be available when needed, that they'll squeak through the window before it closes. This is not a plan, however, this is a hope. In addition, there's another major assumption about Social Security benefits that needs to be challenged: It's the belief that the benefits will be tax-free.

Unfortunately, this may not be true. What *is* true is that if you are single and you have more than $34,000 in other income, then up to 85% of your Social Security income may be subject to taxes. If you are married filing jointly and you have more than $44,000 in other income, it's the same story: Up to 85% of your Social Security Income could be taxable. To develop a better understanding of your taxation of benefits, read IRS Publication 915. You can find it here: http://www.irs.gov/pub/irs-pdf/p915.pdf

Quality of Life

Many of us look ahead to our retirement through rose-colored glasses. We believe we'll be able to travel, live comfortably, and enjoy many of the things we were unable to enjoy during our working years. At a minimum, we believe we'll be able to step off of the treadmill and relax. Often the reality is far different, and by the time we retire and realize the truth it's too late to do much about it. Unfortunately, there are no second chances. When it's our time to retire, we are either ready or not.

The cold hard reality is that, according to Bureau of Labor Statistics, only an estimated 5% of Americans manage to maintain their lifestyle after they retire. What's going on? One huge factor is increasing life expectancy.

Living Longer Costs Money

It's great news that we're living longer: It speaks to the strengths of our society in terms of nutrition, medical care, and so on. But it's clear that we are not, as a nation, financially prepared for our increasing lifespans. By 2016, health spending for each and every person in the nation is expected to hit $11,000 annually, according to the federal government.

Many of us assume that Medicare is comparable in benefits to a good workplace health insurance plan, but that's not the case: It only covers 51% of medical costs. What's more, contrary to widely held belief, Medicare does not pay for long-term care.

And as uncomfortable as it can be to think about, the odds are that you'll need long-term care at some point in your life. About 60% of people over age 65 will eventually require long-term care, according to the Administration on Aging. Long-term care can quickly drain your savings. According to MetLife's 2011 Market Survey of Long-Term Care Costs:

- The national average daily rate for a private room in a nursing home was $239—more than $87,000 annually.

- The average base cost to live in an assisted living community was $3,477 per month, more than $41,000 per year.

In fact, according to a recent study conducted by Fidelity Investments, an average couple retiring in 2012 would need $240,000 just to cover medical costs during retirement. As significant as this amount appears, it doesn't even factor in long-term care expenses.

Our Debt-Driven Society

Debt is a powerful force in the United States. Consumer debt alone helps to drive our economy. As of the end of 2012, the average household owed $23,346 in credit cards, student loans, and other debt. Multiply that by more than 100 million households, and the result is well north of $2 trillion.

It's no mystery why we're up to our necks in debt. According to the Bureau of Economic Analysis, 43% of American families spend more than they earn. The average person spends a whopping 94% of their disposable income, saving a paltry 6%.

Amazingly, just 23% of disposable income goes to the places we'd assume it goes to—food, entertainment, charity, and so on. The rest goes to pay down debt. It's like being on a treadmill with no "off" button.

One reason it's easy to get pulled onto the debt treadmill these days is that debt is cheap. Interest rates continue to hover at all-time lows and that easy credit can be hard to resist. But as your debt adds up, the treadmill seems to spin faster and faster.

While cheap credit is good for borrowing, it's disastrous for savings accounts. Imagine trying to live off of interest of less than 1%. That is today's reality. The same bank that's paying you maybe three-quarters of one percent per year on your savings account might be charging you 8% interest to lend you back that money as part of your mortgage! Nice work if you can get it!

The unfortunate reality is that the average family's savings will never be able to keep pace with the amount of money they give away in the form of interest to traditional lenders. If your savings account can't keep up, though, maybe your investment account can. Isn't that the way to get ahead? Unfortunately, you shouldn't count on it.

The volatility of the investment markets make them a dangerous place to play; the paper profits that you rack up in a bull market can disappear seemingly overnight. At the end of a stomach-churning ride in the stock market, you may be lucky to come out even. In the so-called "lost decade" for stocks, the broad U.S. stock market showed no overall gain for the 10 years ending in 2010. And if you pulled your money to the sidelines at the wrong time during that dismal decade, you may have tallied a significant loss.

The fact is, because of the market's unpredictability, the old assumptions about what you could expect to earn in the stock market, and how long it would take to earn it, have gone out the window. The financial industry has for decades urged us to be patient, "long-term" investors. The market may rise and fall, but over the long term, we've been told, we'll likely enjoy nice gains in the end.

The investment industry has actually changed its definition of long-term investing to fit a changing reality. Most investors aren't aware of this because the industry has done it quietly. But consider this: In the early1980s, a long-term investment was considered to be one that you held on to for one to three years.

When one to three-year performance didn't end up looking as good as anticipated, adjustments were quietly made: Most advisors replaced one-to three-year performance with a three-to-five-year model. These days, most advisors use an illustration of 10 to 20 years in order to show decent rates of return. That raises a question for today's investor. Are you prepared to wait 10, 20, or even 30 years in order to, hopefully, capture a healthy return by speculating in the market?

Clearly, it's time for Americans to change the way we think about our finances and the way we prepare to meet our financial goals. It's time for us to embrace a new financial model.

2

Hope for the Best,
Plan for the Worst

When it comes to our financial well-being, I believe it's time for us to embrace a new paradigm. We must bring to an end the era of relying on the government and on our employers. However well-meaning these institutions may be, reaching our goals is ultimately our own responsibility. With today's uncertainty in the economy and in the markets, it's truer than ever. We simply can't rely on employers or Uncle Sam to take care of us.

It's also time to reevaluate our plan for reaching our financial goals. Relying on the stock market alone to provide a certain rate of return—or relying on real estate or any other speculative investments, for that matter—is an act of faith. There is no guarantee the markets will provide anything like your target rate of return.

Now, it's true the markets can surprise us to the upside *or* to the downside. There may be another bull market around the corner. There may be a bear market in the works. Or the market may just muddle along for years and years. Whatever the case, trying to get a rate of return in the market isn't a plan, it's a hope. Our retirement or other long-term financial plans should not be based simply on hope alone.

In this new world, we must take responsibility for ensuring that we have enough money to last throughout our retirement. Again and again, people who are retired or who are about to retire discover that they have far too little to support themselves in retirement. They can forget about living a dream retirement.

We must make sure that even if we have a sizeable nest egg, it is safe. It can't be subject to the ups and downs of the market. Imagine if you had retired and started drawing down your nest egg at the beginning of the 2000s. You'd be taking out money even as the dot-com crash and the 2008 crisis decimated your savings.

Far too many people found themselves in this exact situation. They had to pull money out of their accounts even when those accounts were shrinking due to market volatility. Today, many of those retirees are in a full-fledged crisis, with their savings crushed and many years of retirement ahead of them.

Expanding Your Financial Toolbox

We've been trained to associate certain financial products with certain goals. For instance, 401(k) plans and IRAs are the way we save for retirement. So-called 529 plans are the way we save for college. We are so used to this limited set of solutions that it can be hard to look beyond them for other options. What about insurance? Many of us equate insurance with protection—protection against financial crises created by illness, disability, or death, for instance. Few are those who understand that insurance can also be a solution for long-term financial goals, including paying for college, buying houses and cars, and even paying for retirement.

No single financial product is a silver bullet for meeting all of your life's financial goals. The truth is that there is a place in solid financial plans for a number of financial products. These products shouldn't be bought and added to your collection willy-nilly, though. It's critical to think about how each product functions and the role that each can play in helping you to reach your particular goals.

Insurance can play a pivotal role in your financial toolbox. But using it requires setting aside a certain mindset that many of us have toward insurance. Too often, we view it as an expense—a good, "responsible" expense, to be sure, but an expense nonetheless. What if you flipped your perception of insurance from being an expense to being an asset? As I'll describe, that is exactly what insurance can be for those who have an open mind about how to use it.

How might insurance fit into your financial toolbox? The answer is that it can be the tool that anchors your overall financial strategy, making the prospect of reaching your goals more certain and less risky. As we prepare for retirement and other long-term goals, we need to be sure that at least a portion of our assets is protected from loss. The right kind of insurance policy can guarantee a safe, predictable rate of return over the years.

How much of your resources should you set aside to gather these safe, predictable returns? That depends on a few key factors, including your specific needs and goals and your risk tolerance. In general, I've learned over my many years of experience that using either whole life or indexed universal life insurance as part of your overall financial plan can be incredibly beneficial.

Plugging Leaks and Taking Control

As an attorney for two decades, I've been privy to some of the most important strategic decisions my clients have faced. When it comes to investing, I've seen clients make the same mistakes over and over again: They buy stocks or real estate as those assets are rising—all the way up to a crash. Then they take their financial advisors' advice to stay the course and wait for the cycle to repeat, over and over again.

Using that rollercoaster as the centerpiece of your financial plan doesn't make any sense. It's far better to rely on a financial solution that can provide steady, predictable, and guaranteed, growth over the years.

The solution is to create your personal banking system using one or more permanent insurance policies. Be advised that the process I describe in this book takes time. It isn't a get-rich-quick scheme. But I have become convinced that it can be an extremely smart alternative to the traditional approach of investing in the stock market, the real estate market, or elsewhere and hoping for a certain rate of return.

The rate of return you can expect through permanent life insurance certainly will not match the best-case scenario in the stock market. However, financial success isn't just about what you earn—it's about what you save. Through your Private Vault, you can avoid paying the fees, service charges, and interest we pay to banks and other lenders. If you're losing less through the financial "leaks" of fees, service charges, and interest, then you can actually earn less on your investment and still come out ahead.

It is essential to remember that the cash-value asset within your permanent life insurance policy is a more valuable asset than many of the alternatives. That's because one of the aspects of an asset's value is its liquidity. Should you need cash at a moment's notice—and this happens all the time in family emergencies—you have it close at hand thanks to your insurance policy.

I have many clients with significant investments in real estate. On paper, they're asset-rich. However, real estate is a non-liquid asset; those clients can't quickly cash out of it if they need to pay for medical expenses, for instance. With a properly designed life insurance policy, on the other hand, policyholders generally have access to cash within a week. That applies to two kinds of insurance that I'll describe in this book: whole life and indexed universal life.

When you set up a personal banking system using insurance, you—not the banks—are in control. You dictate the terms, from how the funds within your insurance will grow, to your ability to access those funds, to how loans taken against those funds are to be repaid.

As a system for funding retirement, your personal banking system has a huge advantage pertaining to taxes. Think about 401(k) plans or even IRAs. They are often described as being "tax-advantaged." Why are they tax-advantaged? Because the federal government allows them to be. Lawmakers have created the terms of those tax advantages, and if lawmakers created them in the first place, they can certainly change them in the future.

Given our country's huge debt, you can be sure that Washington will turn over every stone in the coming years looking for more revenue to pay that debt. It's already raised taxes on dividends and capital gains outside of tax-advantaged products. Will it leave the tax advantages of 401(k)s, IRAs, and similar kinds of accounts alone? I wouldn't bet my retirement on it. Life insurance, on the other hand, takes the government out of the driver's seat when it comes to taxation.

It's a fact that the money you use to fund insurance is not tax-deductible; it's "after-tax" money. By complying with the requirements of IRC Section 7702, insurance benefits are paid out tax-free. Can that change? Can't the government impose new taxes on insurance? The good news is that it cannot. The reason: Life insurance is a private contract between you and your insurance company. It's not a "qualified plan" with the government's seal of approval. Court rulings have affirmed that the government cannot undo the terms of a private contract. From a tax standpoint, you can sleep better at night with an insurance policy than with an investment in the stock market, the bond market, real estate, or a retirement plan.

The Bias against Insurance

It's not hard to find brokers and financial advisors who will casually dismiss the idea of using insurance as a tool to reach your financial goals. Oh sure, they'll agree that you should have term insurance as a safety net to protect your family in the event of your death. But when it comes to using insurance as a way to prepare for retirement, college funding, and other goals, many advisors are simply closed off to the idea. They quickly dismiss it as too expensive and too unorthodox. If personal banks built around insurance are so great, the argument goes, why doesn't everyone have them? Talk about a self-fulfilling argument!

In my opinion, the misinformation used to dismiss insurance stems from an institutional bias that's rooted in Wall Street's goal of hoarding business for itself. It's all about keeping the revenue where they think it belongs—in their pockets.

3

Investing Is *Not* the Same as Saving

I believe that to achieve financial success in our new economy, we have to rethink old assumptions and unexamined beliefs. To move forward, we need to clear out ways of thinking that no longer serve us in the real world. One assumption that is worth reexamining has to do with so-called retirement savings accounts.

We've all heard 401(k)s and IRAs referred to as retirement savings accounts. We've gotten so used to this language that we seldom, if ever, pause to question it. But we all know what a *real* savings account is. Like that first bank account you may have had as a kid, it's a place to safely accumulate money. It's risk-free.

Now think about retirement accounts. The money in those accounts is meant to be invested in the market, which means you can lose your money—theoretically, every penny of it. If you think you're saving for a retirement in a retirement plan, you're off the mark. Realistically, you're using your money to place a bet that the market will rise rather than fall, that your money will increase rather than decrease.

It's possible to keep all your money in cash within a retirement plan, of course. Then you'd really be "saving" for retirement. But that's not the point of retirement accounts. And truth be told, most of us can't really afford to park our retirement funds in cash. For one thing, we need to earn sufficient returns to keep up with inflation. Earning some rate of return above that can mean the difference between meeting our long-term goals or falling short.

I have a client who was so afraid of subjecting his $890,000 nest egg to the market that he kept the entire amount in cash, year after year, within his brokerage account. The problem was that the brokerage firm only paid him $70 annually. That's a return of less than .01%, and it doesn't come close to keeping up with average inflation of 2.5% a year.

Still, one of the fundamental mistakes people make in financial planning is having a conventional retirement plan as its foundation. Tens of millions of Americans are using risky investment accounts, otherwise known as retirement accounts, as though they were risk-free savings accounts. The truth is that we are in a stronger position when the basis of our financial plan is a solution that allows us to grow money without the risk of loss.

Let's take a closer look at why the model of investing your retirement funds in the market is flawed. At the center of it is Wall Street's go-to disclaimer. We've all read or heard it a thousand times: "Past performance is not a guarantee of future results."

But the investment industry seems to operate as if it doesn't quite believe its own disclaimer. All investment portfolio models are created by studying past performance data to try to predict what will happen in the future. How often does that approach work out? Brace yourself: According to John Stossel's 2009 book *Myths, Lies and Downright Stupidity,* fewer than 5% of all professional money managers succeed in matching the return of the S&P 500 index in any one year. And it's never the same 5%, he points out.

What's more, matching the S&P isn't even such a great feat. In a 2010 article on Forbes.com, Michigan-based investment advisor Richard A. Ferri described how over the previous decade, the performance of the index lagged behind every other major asset class.

I believe that regular people understand on some level the truth about investing: that it's a type of gambling. Investment advisors have a handy argument to ease their minds. They assure their clients that they can limit the risk within their portfolios by using diversification.

Diversification involves distributing an investor's money across a wide range of investments—different kinds of assets, different kinds of securities, different kinds of industries. In a nutshell, diversification is sold as the equivalent of putting your eggs in multiple baskets.

Another part of the risk-reduction "science" that investment advisors tout is asset allocation. This involves balancing your investments between the three main asset classes—stocks, bonds, and cash. Each of these asset classes has a different level of risk and return potential, and each is supposed to behave differently over time. In other words, if one asset class is crashing, another should be stable, providing a cushion for your portfolio.

But neither of these strategies—diversification or asset allocation—is sufficient to protect you against what's known as systemic risk. Systemic risk refers to the downturn of the entire market. In that kind of situation, no asset class is safe, and diversification is useless. This is exactly what occurred in the crash of 2008, as the stock market, the bond market, and the real estate market plunged together.

Brokers' and financial advisors' conventional wisdom includes other approaches that are supposed to limit your risk. One of them is dollar-cost averaging. It involves making equal-sized purchases of an investment at set intervals. The upside of this is that if the price of the investment falls over time, you'll essentially be buying shares at a deeper discount each time.

Dollar-cost averaging isn't perfect, though. One criticism is that it can be better to invest your money once, in a lump sum: That way it's at work in the market for a longer period, potentially earning you greater returns. What's more, brokerage fees can add up when you make many investments rather than one.

A staple of financial advisors' wisdom is that investors should exercise discipline, staying the course when markets are volatile. If you remain invested long enough, the reasoning goes, the market and your account balance are bound to recover any losses and then some.

That's true enough in theory. The U.S. economy has grown throughout its history, and the value of the stock market has grown along with it. But the reality is that your financial needs don't always coincide with the direction of the market. What if you're forced to cash out of the market because of life events? Forced retirement is more common than you might think—and it typically happens at the bottom of an economic and market slump. Imagine having to start drawing from your retirement account once it's already down 20%! That sort of reality can throw the best-laid plains about funding retirement into disarray.

There's another risk of using a conventional investment account to fund your retirement and it has to do with human emotions. A recent study by research firm Dalbar, Inc., found that the S&P 500 index returned 8.35% on average over

the 20 years ending in 2008. But the average equity investor earned a mere 1.87%. That return wasn't even enough to
keep up with the period's inflation rate of 2.89%.

Bond investors were in the same boat. Their returns over
that same two-decade period were a paltry 0.77%, compared
with a return of 7.43% for the Barclay's Capital Aggregate
Bond Index. The reason for this performance gap is simple:
Investors are human, and humans are driven by their emotions. Acting out of our primal emotions of fear and greed, we
sell when we should stay invested, and we buy when investments are at their most expensive.

It's true that the market has always risen over the long
term. But capturing those gains requires a self-discipline most
investors simply don't have.

Playing With Numbers

The investment industry—the mutual fund business in
particular—uses a self-serving way of expressing investment
returns. If you read the fine print of just about any ad touting a
hot-performing fund, you'll notice the term "average return."
Average return is a simple calculation, but a potentially
misleading one. To get it, you add up the annual returns of a
fund or other investment and divide by the number of years.

A more accurate way to express returns is as "real returns."
To get the real return, add or subtract each year's performance
figures as you go along. That means adding or subtracting
each year's return so you start each new year with the new
value.

It's very likely that any fund's real return will be less than
the average return if the fund's track record includes any years
with a loss. If the fund has had only positive returns, then

its average return will likely be higher than its real return. The bottom line is that the way the investment industry plays with numbers, the actual amount of money you make over the years may well be less than the returns you've supposedly earned.

Is the market the only way to get the returns that you need to meet your financial goals? We've all been brainwashed with the idea that we have to invest in the market in order to earn adequate returns. The investment industry focuses on best-case outcomes and doesn't say much about the possibility of worst-case outcomes, specifically market losses. Investors are left to hope for the best, usually without being prepared for the worst.

Rarely are investors warned about the merciless math of the market: It's easier to lose money than it is to earn it back. A simple example is that if you lose 10%, you'll need to earn 11% just to get back to even.

A 10% LOSS REQUIRES AN 11% GAIN TO ALMOST BREAK EVEN

Principal	10% Loss	10% Gain After Loss
$100	$90	$99

Principal	10% Loss	11% Gain After Loss
$100	$90	$99.90

The Investment Industry's View of Insurance

Most advisors won't deign to consider the idea of using insurance as an investment vehicle. Their mantra is the almost knee-jerk phrase: "Buy term and invest the difference." In a nutshell, that means you should buy term insurance to protect your family against the risk of your death. The rationale is that since term insurance is much cheaper than the permanent life insurance that accumulates a cash value, you can take the money you'll save and invest it.

The "buy term and invest the difference" argument is based on some shaky assumptions, however. The first is that the market will deliver consistent returns without any loss to your capital. Properly structured permanent life insurance, as you'll learn, will guarantee you a rate of return. But investing in the market, outside of an annuity, comes with no guarantee whatsoever that you'll earn a rate of return and that your underlying capital will be safe.

Another dubious assumption is that once they buy a term insurance policy, policyholders will actually invest the difference. In many cases, they won't invest it, and won't even save it—they'll spend it. It takes a lot of discipline to do otherwise.

Relying on term insurance has an additional flaw. Since term insurance by definition expires after a specified period, purchasing it assumes we won't need coverage after it expires. In fact, the opposite is often true: Our term insurance expires when we are older and statistically more likely to die. Remember, the older we are when our term insurance expires, the harder is it to qualify for new term insurance, and the more expensive that insurance becomes. Too many people have had their term insurance expire at age 65, for instance, and found themselves without life insurance despite having paid hundreds or thousands of dollars over the years.

Those who've tried to renew their term insurance in their 60s can attest to the fact that it's prohibitively expensive to do so. And that's for those in good health. (As you'll learn in more detail later in the book, one of the great advantages of embarking now on a financial plan based on permanent life insurance is that you will never have to worry about obtaining it—you'll have it, as the name indicates, permanently.)

In an illogical practice, term policyholders are typically advised to cancel their policies when their kids are grown or their house is paid off. The idea is that the cash freed up by those events can replace the insurance coverage. This isn't a wise choice in my opinion. Losing the policy's death benefit amounts to intentionally reducing the assets that may be available to your spouse or children. It's a fact that we will all die some day. And when we do, we should have insurance in place so our beneficiaries are placed in the best position possible to move forward.

The investment industry has a few staple arguments against the use of permanent insurance. A favorite is that the costs of whole life policies are front-loaded. It's true that costs associated with the death benefit, the fees for administration, and the insurance agent's sales fee are paid early in the policy, but within this argument is usually the unstated message that the fees aren't fair.

In fact, each fee represents something of value for the permanent life customer. Administrative fees are spent setting up and maintaining the policy. Insurance agents are compensated for their investment in explaining, researching, and customizing a policy according to each customer's specific needs. When you pay death benefit costs, you are investing in an extremely valuable asset for your spouse, kids, or other beneficiaries.

Furthermore, if these policies are used as intended, the question of when those costs are paid is not really relevant. In reality, it's not only true that costs are front-loaded, but it's also true that several years of funding are required before a permanent life policy can start to be used as a personal banking solution.

But after those first several years, the benefits you'll enjoy can begin to match, and eventually outweigh, the costs. Your personal banking system will then continue to benefit you for years and even decades after those up-front costs have been paid. On top of that, your beneficiary will have access to a substantial death benefit.

Critics of permanent life also like to argue that it takes 15 years until the premiums paid into a policy equal the policy's cash value. This assertion is misleading; the 15-year scenario is only accurate for policies that are not designed for maximum accumulation of cash value. In a policy properly designed for your personal banking system, cash value should match premium contributions in half that time or less.

Incidently, policies that aren't designed for cash accumulation often make perfect sense. What the naysayers tend to leave unsaid is that, even in their scenarios, cash value will ultimately exceed the premiums. Those critics also conveniently overlook just how valuable a policy's death benefit is. It's not surprising those with competing interests fail to judge permanent insurance even-handedly: it's not in their interest to do so.

Many financial advisors also tell their clients that better returns are available by investing outside the policy. Again, investing in the market is the business those folks are in, so it's not surprising that they'd have an optimistic outlook. But their faith in the market is just that—faith. It's not a guarantee. As we've discussed, investing in the market over the long term can be like walking over a tightrope to your destination: Your capital is vulnerable along the way, to everything from market losses to fees and taxes.

Could you do better by taking your chances in the market rather than accepting guaranteed modest returns within an insurance policy? It's absolutely possible. But it's just as possible to be disappointed, as countless investors can attest. By inviting us to invest in the market as the foundation of our financial plans, advisors are asking us to rely on an approach that is intrinsically unreliable.

4

Beware of
Conventional Wisdom

W all Street and the banks peddle the conventional wisdom about financial planning because it benefits them to do so. That can hurt clients in big and small ways. If you take a step back, you can see that financial institutions herd us into a few selective investment solutions—all of which have serious limitations. Unfortunately, once we're in these products, it can be extremely hard to get out. Who does this conventional approach benefit? Overwhelmingly, it benefits Wall Street and the banks.

Consider the ways your hands are tied with a product like a 401(k). Right off the bat, you're informed that there are restrictions on funding: You can contribute as much as the government says you can contribute, based on your age. If you're younger, you can't contribute as much as older participants.

Other rules include the fact that you must have earned income at least equal to the amount you contribute in a given year. This can hinder planning for children and grandchildren because gifts to children's or grandchildren's retirement plans are not permitted unless they meet the earned-income test. Being unable to make gifts can remove a long-term wealth planning option for those you care about.

Another big drawback of 401(k)s is their lack of investment control. Participants may think they're in charge because they get to pick the investments within their 401(k) account. The reality is that when you choose investments, you are choosing from a limited menu of options that is dictated by your plan's custodian.

Whatever investments you choose, they're likely to be mutual funds, which are the only option available to most 401(k) participants. There are more than 20,000 mutual funds, but again, plan participants have access to just a handful that are selected for them. The truth is that 401(k) participants' main choice is "take it or leave it."

401(k) Winners and Losers

Financial institutions are content with this arrangement because it's simple and profitable for them. And a dependable stream of fees makes it a golden goose. Think about it: The "advisors" who administer 401(k)s have a captive "customer" base who are regularly adding assets to the plans. The greater the assets within a plan, the more administrators stand to earn. Don't forget the government: 401(k)s may be "tax advantaged," but when all is said and done, Uncle Sam ultimately gets a hefty cut through taxes. Again, the greater the total assets within plans such as 401(k)s, the more revenue the government rakes in.

It's often said that the real way to make a killing on Wall Street is not to put your money into investments, but to sell those investments. That's true in spades when it comes to

401(k)s. They provide a stream of fee income that's irresistible to financial institutions. But what do those fees—paid out of your pocket—mean to you?

Most 401(k) participants don't realize it, but the annual management fees they pay may be as high as 3%. It's hard enough to earn the kind of solid return that you need to reach your retirement goals. Now imagine that you're losing 3% off the top each and every year! It's been shown that fees of even 2% per year can reduce your long-term return by half. It's no wonder so many 401(k) "retirement savers" struggle to prepare for retirement. It's almost as if they're the proverbial sucker at the poker table.

It would be nice if investors had as much certainty about their expected returns as administrators have about their annual fee income. However, investing in the market, through 401(k)s or other routes, is an inherently unpredictable business. The market has always fluctuated and always will, and that means it's impossible to be sure how much money we'll have available for our retirement.

Another huge uncertainty surrounding 401(k)s has to do with taxes. Contrary to what many of us have been told, individuals often find themselves in a higher tax bracket in retirement. And many people are surprised to learn that retirement income is distributed as ordinary taxable income.

Retirement income is often taxed in a higher bracket than recipients expect because of the deductions that retirees tend to have lost. If you've followed widespread advice and paid off your mortgage, you lose your mortgage interest deduction. Since your children will be grown, you won't be able to claim them as dependents for tax purposes.

There's more: Since you'll most likely no longer have earned income, you won't be eligible to make tax-deductible contributions to retirement plans. This uncertainty around your tax bracket makes the tax benefits of 401(k)s much less appealing.

What's more, getting access to those supposed tax advantages involves a huge tradeoff: locking up your money, possibly for decades. Part of the value of money lies in being able to use it whenever you need it. With 401(k)s, it's almost as though the money isn't really yours until a certain point in your life.

Access to your money is restricted by both the government and employers. You can expect to pay taxes and a stiff 10% penalty to the IRS if you need to withdraw your money prior to age 59½.

There is an "escape hatch" exception to this rule, known as a Section 72(t) distribution. This approach comes with its own strict set of rules: You must use your life expectancy to calculate "substantially equal" annual distributions, and once those distributions begin, they must continue for five years or until you reach age 59½, whichever is longer.

On the other hand, if you don't need your 401(k) money, keeping it in your account isn't an option. By law, mandatory distributions must begin at age 70½. Failing to begin taking those distributions means you will be subject to a 100% excise tax. Even if you don't want your money, the government wants *its* tax money!

Now for your employer's restrictions. If you're currently employed, your company may have the ability to prevent you from tapping your 401(k), even if you're older than 59½. Most people who are subject to this restriction aren't even aware of it because it's buried in the fine print of their 401(k) paperwork. If you didn't think companies could use 401(k)s as "golden handcuffs," you now know otherwise.

AVOID 10% EARLY WITHDRAWAL PENALTY 72T ELECTION

Age	Withdrawal	Ending Balance
55	$12,862	$248,995
56	$12,862	$247,940
57	$12,862	$246,831
58	$12,862	$245,668
59	$12,862	$244,446

*These figures are estimates based upon a hypothetical growth rate of 5% and a 3% distribution rate.

IRAs: A Better Alternative?

What about IRAs? Unfortunately, they have most of the same drawbacks as 401(k)s. Plus, they are subject to additional restrictions on tax deductibility depending on earned income and on whether you participate in a qualified plan.

Roth IRAs, which are funded with after-tax income, may help to address the issue of being in a higher tax bracket in retirement. But they involve plenty of "cons" too. One of the main downsides involves restrictions on funding. As with 401(k) plans, IRA holders face contribution limits based on age. Additionally, the same equivalent-earned-income rule applies, which can throw a wrench into planning for children and grandchildren.

Roth IRAs are also restricted based on income limits: if you earn more than a certain threshold, you lose your ability to contribute. In a prime example of a "marriage penalty," that threshold is actually lower for families with joint income. For those who are eligible, Roth IRAs do grow tax-free, since you've already paid taxes when the funds were contributed. That tax-free growth comes with the all-too familiar restrictions about accessing your capital.

To qualify for a tax-free withdrawal, your distribution must occur at least five years after you established and funded the Roth IRA. Although there are exceptions, the system is designed so that you can generally get your money only upon turning 59½.

It is time to look at some of the other conventional financial solutions that banks and Wall Street urge their clients to use. First we will expand on mutual funds. In 2011, more than 52 million U.S. households owned mutual funds, according to the 2012 Investment Company Fact Book.

Incredible Shrinking Returns

Mutual funds do come with a number of handy selling points, and none is talked about more than diversification. The idea is that professional mutual fund managers spread your money around in different stocks and bonds to take advantage of opportunities and hedge against trouble. However, you already know that mutual funds come with no guarantees and are built on models of what has worked in the past. Even those that invest successfully involve a major flaw: Their diversification and other features come at a steep cost.

Whether your mutual fund tanks or shoots the lights out, one thing remains constant—you continue paying costly fees.

Most mutual fund investors understand that they're paying an expense ratio for fund management and other costs. Unfortunately they're often oblivious to the laundry list of fees associated with their investments. "Loads," or up-front sales charges, can immediately chop as much as 8.5% off your investment capital. Then investors pay layer after layer of fees, from transaction costs to services charges to fees for receiving paper statements.

Funds are supposed to disclose the lengthy list of fees in their public documents, and if you dare to wade through the legalese you can find them there. Unfortunately, some fees are nearly invisible. Specifically, funds that buy and sell frequently can rack up higher tax burdens for shareholders. The typical mutual fund is like Grand Central Station, with new stocks coming in and old ones departing. In fact, the average fund "turnover" is a full 85% of its portfolio each year. Selling a stock sooner than one year after buying it triggers short-term capital gains taxes, which are quietly passed on to the investor.

Mutual fund returns are often bandied about as if the entire return goes directly into your pocket. But thanks to taxes, this isn't necessarily so. Once the IRS aims its shrink ray at your returns, you may be surprised at how little you're able to keep.

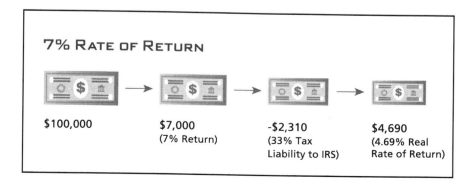

7% RATE OF RETURN

$100,000 → $7,000 (7% Return) → -$2,310 (33% Tax Liability to IRS) → $4,690 (4.69% Real Rate of Return)

Imagine you are in the 33% tax bracket, and your taxable mutual fund has a 7% return. After the IRS takes its 2.31%, your real return is just 4.69%. And that's not counting those short-term capital gains taxes.

The "Safe" Route

You can avoid risks and certain fees by going the "safe" route of stashing your money in a bank certificate of deposit or savings account. With interest rates at extreme lows, that's almost the equivalent of stuffing cash into your mattress.

The idea of safety, however, is so powerful that a surprising number of people still choose this approach. They stash their money away, then use the cash for purchases. What they fail to recognize is that this system carries a large cost in terms of lost opportunity.

It seems compelling and even virtuous to use cash for purchases, but this is another area where it can pay to reexamine our ingrained beliefs.

If we step back, we can see that many of us are caught in a cycle of saving money, then depleting those funds to make purchases. This cycle means that after each purchase, we must start over from square one, saving for the next purchase. Once we use our savings, the funds are gone forever, and they're generally used to buy assets that depreciate in value over the years. The bottom line is that the system of saving and spending depletes our wealth, or at a minimum keeps it from accumulating. Later in this book I will discuss an alternative to this way of thinking—an alternative that can help you to make all the purchases you normally would while building wealth in the process.

College Savings Plans

They've only been around since 1996, but "529" college savings plans reached $190.7 billion in assets in 2012, an increase of about 16% from the prior year. The plans have caught on in large part because of the inflation in college costs. Tuition costs have long increased an average of 5% a year, and they are expected to more than double over the next 15 years.

College savings plans are designed to help families pay for their kids' education. As with Roth IRAs, contributions to 529 plans are not tax-deductible, although the funds can eventually be withdrawn tax-free.

How Much Will a College Education Cost?

Approximate Undergraduate Charges (2012-2013) to Attend a Four-Year College:

— PUBLIC SCHOOL

- **Annual Cost:**
  Resident Student* $17,860
  Commuter Student** $8,655

— PRIVATE SCHOOL

- **Annual Cost:**
  Resident Student* $39,518
  Commuter Student** $29,056

* Includes tuition, fees, room and board; in-state residency is assumed for public schools.

** Includes tuition and fees only.

Source: The College Board Trends in College Pricing 2012

Note: While these are the average published tuition, fee and room and board charges, many students actually pay less due to grant aid and federal tax benefits.

Years Until College	4-Year Total Cost	
	PUBLIC	**PRIVATE**
1	$80,828.00	$178,844.00
2	$84,869.00	$187,786.00
3	$89,112.00	$197,175.00
4	$93,568.00	$207,034.00
5	$98,246.00	$217,386.00
6	$103,158.00	$228,255.00
7	$108,316.00	$239,668.00
8	$113,732.00	$251,651.00
9	$119,419.00	$264,234.00
10	$125,390.00	$277,446.00
11	$131,660.00	$291,318.00
12	$138,243.00	$305,884.00
13	$145,050.00	$321,178.00
14	$152,303.00	$337,237.00
15	$159,918.00	$354,099.00

Based on the College Board's Trends in College Pricing 2012, which estimates average annual costs of $17,860 at public colleges and $39,518 at private nonprofit colleges (includes tuition, fees, room and board). In-state residency is assumed for public schools. Table assumes 5% annual increase in college costs and a 7% after-tax annual return on investment, based on monthly compounding. No additional investments are assumed once the child starts college.

Just because 529 plans are increasingly popular doesn't mean they're perfect—far from it. First of all, similar to 401(k) "retirement savings plans," their name is a misnomer: 529 plans are investment vehicles, not savings vehicles. Investors in the plans can theoretically lose every penny of their capital.

In volatile markets, investors may be *unable* to keep from losing money. That's because funds within the plans can only be reallocated between mutual funds once a year. In other words, you can shift from conservative to risky funds, but if markets tank, you're potentially trapped for many months in those risky funds.

The whole point of 529 plans is to grow your capital so there's enough to pay for college. But what if the money doesn't grow, or doesn't grow enough? Or what if you lose capital? In that case the money you'd counted on to pay college expenses isn't available, and you're in a bind.

As with other "tax-advantaged" investment vehicles, there's the saying "the IRS giveth and the IRS taketh away." In this case, what's taken away is control over the funds within your plan. The funds must be used for college-related expenses. If they're withdrawn and used for any other purpose, they're subject to a 10% penalty.

Furthermore, the designated recipients of the funds must withdraw them for college-related expenses by age 30. If they fail to do so, the funds are distributed to the recipients regardless of their wishes, and subjected to a 10% penalty. Now, most of us want our kids to graduate from college, but many people succeed without a college degree—do the names Bill Gates and Steve Jobs ring a bell? The fact is that 529 plans strip their intended recipients of the flexibility to choose a non-traditional path.

Conventional Wisdom on Mortgages

One of the bedrock assumptions I've heard from client after client over the years has to do with the importance of paying off your home. Paying off your home as soon as possible, the thinking goes, is critical to achieving financial security. Probably the biggest motivation for those who strive to pay off their homes is a desire to break free of the power of their mortgage lender. Once you've paid off your mortgage, after all, the bank can't foreclose on you.

The instinct to own your home free and clear is easy for everyone to understand on a gut level. But when it comes to the subject of mortgages, it's worthwhile to take a step back and do some critical thinking. What might it cost you to pay off your home sooner than you need to? Does an all-out assault on your mortgage make sense if it comes at the cost of other priorities? We can all agree, for example, that owning your home outright will be little comfort if you can't afford groceries or fuel for your car in retirement.

Let's look at the idea that homeowners are at their lenders' mercy until they pay off their mortgages. Our grandparents and great-grandparents lived in an era in which their bank could "call" their mortgage at any time. Even if the homeowner had a spotless repayment record, the lender could decide at the drop of a hat that they had to repay the loan immediately. This is exactly what took place in the Great Depression era. Fortunately, laws have long since been put in place to make it illegal for banks to call your mortgage as they could back then.

Yet even today, decades after calling mortgages on responsible borrowers was outlawed, countless homeowners sacrifice month after month in an effort to pay off their mortgage as quickly as possible. Talk about the need to reexamine your assumptions and beliefs! These folks are acting based on a system that vanished more than seven decades ago!

This continued behavior is a testament to the power of fear in driving humans' decisions. I'd like to challenge you to make decisions based not in fear but in reality.

Now, banks certainly don't discourage their borrowers from "paying ahead" on their mortgages. The reason should come as no surprise: Lenders benefit from those extra payments. In simple terms, the faster you pay off your debt, the better position you put your lender in.

One of the main risks that mortgage lenders face is borrowers' inability to continue payments because of job loss, illness, or other unexpected problems. If you've paid your debt at an accelerated rate prior to a foreclosure, the bank has recouped more of its loan that it otherwise would have. Your diligence in paying ahead has served as a kind of free insurance for the bank, limiting the loss it might absorb on a loan that stops "performing."

It's natural for many of us to think of our home as an investment. But if you think about it, a home in some ways is the opposite of an investment. Most of us use mortgages to buy our homes. A mortgage, of course, is a loan that is based purely upon your income. It doesn't reflect the equity in your home.

That equity—the amount of principal you've paid on your loan—generates a goose-egg rate of returning a whopping: 0%.

What's more, the equity in your home isn't really useful. If you own 100 shares of Google, you always have the option of selling those shares, effectively exchanging them for cash in hand within a matter of days. But what if you need access to the "equity" in your house for an emergency?

Well, if you're considered a good credit risk, you might get a home equity loan within a matter of weeks. By then, your crisis may have passed—for better or worse. And what if your credit rating is no longer in great shape? That equity in your home is likely to remain locked up where you have no access to it.

Let's look at the way that many financially secure people think about paying for homes. It may seem strange at first when you see people who have the means to pay off their homes quickly choose not to do so. These folks have sized up the situation logically and realized a few key facts:

- Their homes are safe. They know that as long as they keep up with payments, their lenders can't touch their property.

- There's a big benefit to having a mortgage. Specifically, mortgage interest is one of the best tax deductions available to the wealthy.

- There are greener pastures. Savvy homeowners understand that making minimal mortgage payments allows them to direct their extra resources toward more lucrative opportunities.

In fact, savvy folks understand that mortgage debt can be a profitable financial tool. Over time, mortgage payments result in more and more equity in our homes. If that equity is just accrued and left alone, it doesn't serve us. If we extract our equity over time, in the form of home equity loans, and put it to use wisely, in the long run we may come out way ahead.

Keeping equity in your home relatively low can also be a smart way to protect your assets from creditors and lawsuits. The key is a legal protection known as the Homestead Exemption. All states have a version of the Homestead Exemption, which specifies the amount of equity you can have in your home without the home being subject to attachment in a lawsuit.

For example, if you live in Washington State and have less than $125,000 in equity, your home is protected.

Our Money under Siege

When it comes to our financial future, we're surrounded by uncertainty. The solutions that the financial industry and the government push us toward only compound that uncertainty, and all the while the unyielding forces of taxes and inflation are quietly eroding our wealth.

Taxes hit us from all sides and can turn our supposed income into fiction. We don't just pay taxes to the IRS, after all. Most of us pay state income taxes, too. Then there are sales taxes, use taxes, and all kinds of hidden taxes. Sometimes our taxes are used to pay for things that literally do not exist: In my hometown of Seattle, we are still paying off the Kingdome, which opened in 1976 and was demolished in 2000!

Taxes and inflation combine to reduce our buying power, and they're hurting us more and more as our average lifespan grows longer and longer. The good news is that you can embark on a better path than conventional wisdom offers. You can plan now for long-term growth of your capital that will generate tax-free access to cash throughout your lifetime.

5

The Consumer Culture

Every one of us is on a path that we hope will lead to financial success. Whether your idea of success is buying an island or simply being able to retire without outliving your savings, each of us has a destination that we're consciously or unconsciously navigating toward.

As we strive to reach our financial goals, we encounter an incredible amount of drag on a day-to-day basis. For most of us the reason is very simple: it's as if we're running a race—but carrying a banker on our back every step of the way!

The Financing Trap

We all know that we live in a consumer society. Just about every material thing we could ever want is easily within our reach. What's more, whether it's a car, a house, or a vacation, we aren't even required to pay for it at the time we buy it—that's what credit cards and bank loans are for! We have been conditioned to view ourselves as consumers, and to use credit to obtain the things we want. It's as natural to us as breathing air.

We all know that paying interest is the cost of having *what we want, when we want it.* The truth is we're usually most concerned about high-interest loans and credit cards. Countless Americans who have scored low-interest mortgages in the recent low-rate environment think of themselves as lucky.

Yet our practice of financing transactions can have a devastating impact over the years on our ability to reach our long-term goals and achieve financial freedom. When I use the analogy of running a race with a banker on your back, I'm not kidding.

Think about the last time you bought a car. You probably reached out to a bank or other lender and jumped through a series of hoops needed for loan approval. You filled out all the necessary paperwork, the lender determined that your credit rating was acceptable, and you were finally approved for your loan.

Documents Needed for Auto Loan Qualification

- Proof of Income
- Credit & Banking History
- Proof of Residence
- Proof of Insurance

Your lending institution called all the shots. It dictated that you were only allowed to use the funds to buy a car. It informed you of the interest rate you'd be paying, the fees you'd be charged, and the schedule you'd need to follow to repay the loan. It even reserved the right to repossess the car if you failed to meet the terms of the agreement.

Even as you drove your newly purchased car home, you'd begun the cycle of paying principal, interest, and fees to your lender. You look forward to paying off the loan—and yet you usually need a new car well before that final loan payment is in sight. That's how it works for most of us: We live on a financial treadmill with no "off" switch, paying month after month of interest and fees, which, of course, are lost to us forever.

FINANCING A VEHICLE

— Borrow $40k

- 5-year Term at 3%
- $3,140 in Interest Paid
- Total Payments of **$43,140**

Now, you may be one of those people who have the discipline to "pay as you go." You don't rely on financing to make purchases because you want to avoid paying interest and fees. That's smart as far as it goes. Let's look more closely at the costs of saving for purchases.

Savers start from scratch and gradually put away money until they've accumulated enough to buy that car in cash. It feels great to drive off the lot free and clear. However, buying that car means the savings are gone. The saver then starts from scratch once more, accumulating funds for his next major purchase. The saver is caught in his own vicious cycle—continually building and depleting savings.

Because those savings must remain liquid, and can't be put at risk in the investment market, they don't grow, and they may not even keep pace with inflation. What's more, once the saver empties his account to pay for his next car, or house, or vacation, that person has no money on which to potentially earn interest or capital gains.

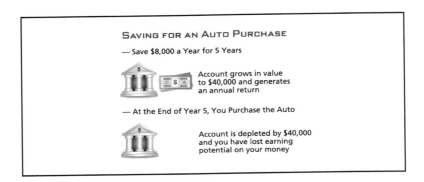

Fortunately, there is a better alternative to both the "financing" and the "saving" approaches.

Opportunity Cost

When you spend a dollar, you are making not one but two choices: You are choosing what to spend that dollar on, and you are choosing not to use it for other purposes. A simple example is buying a car. By using cash to buy a car, you are forgoing the opportunity to keep that cash and potentially earn interest on it over many years.

This dynamic is at the center of a concept that is well worth understanding because it can be the key to your achieving financial independence. The concept is "Economic Value Added," and it's one that businesses have been using to their advantage for years.

Prior to the concept of Economic Value Added, or EVA, businesses were accustomed to investing capital back into the various parts of their companies in order to help them grow. EVA recognizes that there is a "cost" to using capital for internal investment, namely the opportunity cost of not deploying that money in potentially more profitable ways.

Businesses using the EVA concept don't just "give" their capital to their operating units and trust that the investments will lead to increased revenue. They insist that those operating units generate a return on the capital that is greater than what it could return if put to other uses. By recognizing that capital has an inherent value, businesses are able to deploy it to its fullest potential.

The same principle applies to individuals and families. Think about the example from a moment ago of financing a car. Now imagine that, instead of financing the car through a bank or other lender, you finance it through your own "bank"—your Private Vault. Here is what you will have accomplished once you've paid off your loan:

- You will have recouped the interest paid on the loan (after all, you're the "banker," so you receive the benefit of the interest payments).

- You will have replenished every penny of principal back to your Private Vault.

- You will have a fully paid-up asset.

Will your asset have depreciated in value? Of course. But it would have depreciated just the same if you'd financed through an outside lender. By acting as your own banker, you have increased your wealth, not someone else's. You have turned opportunity cost to your advantage. By paying for the asset *and* paying yourself that money right back, you have managed to have your cake and eat it too.

Let's use the example of purchasing a car to break down the options we have when it comes to using our funds in ways that can increase our wealth and help us meet our long-term financial goals:

Option 1: Financing. When you finance your car, you pay interest and fees to your bank or other lender—money that is lost to you forever. When the loan is paid off, all you're left with is a depreciating asset in your garage.

Option 2: Paying Cash. This approach permanently costs you the opportunity to earn interest on your funds. In fact, since your car will depreciate in value, the approach guarantees you a loss.

Option 3: Financing and investing. Some folks who have the cash to buy their car outright opt to finance the car anyway, and invest their cash. They figure that they can earn a return greater than the interest rate and fees they'll pay for the car. But coming out ahead requires a high rate of return on your investment. Of course, investing in the markets can result in loss—often when you invest more aggressively in the hopes of earning a big return.

Option 4: Using your Private Vault. By using your private banking system to finance a car, you ultimately recoup all of the principal, as well as the interest that would have otherwise gone to the bank on the corner. You have your car, and you have built wealth for yourself.

Understanding Insurance Companies

This book is about using permanent life insurance policies as the mechanism to create your Private Vault. To be open to this method of growing and managing your wealth, it's necessary to be confident that insurance companies are strong, reliable institutions. Before we go further, let's take a look at how insurance companies work. One very instructive way to do that is to compare them with banks.

We usually think of banks as a necessary part of our society. The truth is that banks need us more than we need them. You and I, after all, are their source of cheap capital.

U.S. banks operate under what's known as a fractional reserve system. Banks are required to keep a fraction of your deposits on reserve. This is generally 10%, or $1 of every $10 that you and other depositors give to the bank. What do banks do with the other $9? They lend it back to us to finance houses, cars, and other purchases. They lend us back our *own* money!

Naturally, if all of a bank's depositors requested to withdraw their money at the same time, the bank couldn't deliver the money. Still, except in rare cases of "runs" on a bank, this doesn't happen. Customers' withdrawals are offset by deposits and loan repayments that are made in the same timeframe.

What do banks do with their reserve funds—that 10% of deposits that isn't to be lent out? Those funds, known as Tier One Capital, serve as a cushion to protect banks during challenging times. By law, Tier One Capital cannot be invested in the stock market, which is deemed too risky.

Tier One Capital must consist of what bank regulators deem to be the most safe and liquid assets. Which assets are safe enough to make the cut? Well, they include cash, precious metals, loans from the federal government, and bank-owned life insurance. Take note: Life insurance is considered so safe that it's allowed to make up part of Tier One Capital, a linchpin of our nation's entire banking system.

That brings us to life insurance companies. One of the reasons life insurance is considered such a safe, solid investment has to do with the structure of the insurance companies. Life insurers operate under a different set of regulations than banks, and they use a completely different funding system.

Insurance companies are not permitted to use a fractional reserve system. Because they pay out large death benefits every day, they are required to maintain adequate reserves to pay those claims. Additionally, insurance companies must maintain reserves to meet all guaranteed minimum interest-rate calculations. To do so, they must identify and use safe, conservative investments for their funds.

- When an insurance company has $100 million in potential obligations, it must set aside $100 million to satisfy those obligations.

- When a bank has $100 million in deposits, it must set aside $10 million to satisfy customer withdrawals.

As you can see, insurance companies and banks are fundamentally and structurally different in how they operate. Banks, through the fractional reserve system, are leveraged against their deposits. It's no surprise that, just since 2000, several hundred U.S. banks have failed or been forced to merge into other banks. When is the last time you heard of an insurance company failing?

To the contrary, our country's insurance companies have an extremely consistent record, spanning the past two hundred years, of meeting their obligations. They've reliably paid claims through the booms and busts of the economy and the markets. Banks and other lenders are well aware of this; it's why they depend upon insurance companies to insure the collateral used to back loan agreements.

6

Understanding Insurance Options

Specific types of life insurance are required to set up your private banking system. This chapter will discuss which kinds of insurance you can use to create your Private Vault and which kinds you can't.

Term Life Insurance

In the insurance industry, there's a tongue-in-cheek saying about term life insurance: "You only win if you die." That's more than a joke—it's term life in a nutshell.

There's no cash-value component with term life. It's simply a contract covering a certain term—typically 10 to 30 years. If you die during the term of the policy, your beneficiaries are paid a death benefit. In other words, you, or rather they, "win," and the insurer "loses."

With term life, you're placing a bet that you'll die before the end of the term, and the insurance company is placing a bet that you won't. Can you guess who usually wins the bet?

Insurance companies, of course. Less than 1% of term insurance policies actually pay out; 99% of the time, the insurers win.

- Take Mary for example. In the year 2000, when Mary was 35, she decided to purchase a 10-year term policy to provide for her children, with an annual premium payment of $5,000. When Mary turned 45, she was quite happy that she hadn't died, but the $50,000 she'd paid the insurance company for coverage had completely disappeared. Unfortunately, since the policy had terminated at the end of the 10-year period, Mary had to start all over—and because she was now 10 years older, she had to pay higher premiums for the same coverage.

Term insurance is extremely profitable for insurance companies. As a rule, the longer the term of an insurance policy, the more expensive it is (and the more lucrative for the insurer). Term insurance is what's known as "pure insurance": There is no cash buildup in the policies—they are strictly a bet on your life.

As we discussed in Chapter 4, the financial sector typically advises people to avoid insurance that has a cash-value component. Their mantra is to buy the cheaper form of insurance (term) and invest the money saved. But the "buy term and invest the difference" advice has some major flaws.

First of all, most people don't follow through and invest the difference in the market. It's simply human nature to spend the savings rather than invest it. But even if term policyholders do "invest the difference," doing so is no guarantee that they'll earn a return. In fact, a significant market downturn could result in a loss. By contrast, the cash-value component of permanent life insurance can provide a consistent rate of return.

- How would Mary have fared if she had invested her $50,000 directly in the S&P 500 from 2000 to 2010? During those years, Mary would have experienced six years of positive returns. Unfortunately for Mary, the S&P was down four years, and at the end of the decade, the value of the original $50,000 investment would have dropped 9%, to $45,500. To make matters worse, if Mary had died during this period, there would be no insurance coverage in place for her children.

In guiding you toward term insurance and away from whole life insurance, advisors usually point out that you only need insurance until a certain age. It protects your family from being swamped with bills in the event of your death, the reasoning goes. However, buying term assumes that you'll be able to pay off all of your expenses before the policy expires.

The reality is that in many cases, term policies expire at inconvenient times—before your home is paid off or before your kids have graduated from college, for instance. And what happens when you try to renew the policy or buy a new one? Well, since term premium levels are based on your age, you'll find that you'll have to pay significantly more every month to do so. In insurance companies' eyes, the older you are, the more likely you are to die, and thus the more likely it is that they'll have to make a payout. Thus, they charge you more.

Renewing or starting a new term policy has additional drawbacks. Prohibitive cost is one possible scenario, and another is, quite frankly, that you may no longer be insurable—you may have an illness that will disqualify you.

- If Mary had become ill during her 10-year term period, she may have become ineligible to either renew her term insurance or purchase a new policy.

In buying term insurance, you are making the decision that your family won't need access to a death benefit after your policy has expired. Is term cheaper than other forms of life insurance? Yes. But the way it almost always plays out is that term policyholders pay their insurance companies thousands of dollars and die after the covered term with nothing to show for their investment.

Insurance companies created a work around to this problem by developing what is known as a return-of-premium rider. You will pay additional money for this rider, but at the end of your term policy the money you have paid the insurance company will be returned to you. In effect, you are hedging your bet in case you do not die during the period of coverage. While it is nice to receive your premium payments back, you need to understand how much more in premiums you will be paying under such a rider, and also understand the eroding effect inflation will have had on your money when the premiums are returned to you at the end of coverage.

In any event, because term life has no cash-value component, it can't be used to establish a private banking system—your Private Vault.

Whole Life Insurance

Now let's take a look at whole life insurance. I'll focus on whole life insurance issued by mutual insurance companies. These mutual, or "participating" companies are owned by their policyholders. Unlike publicly traded companies, whose employees ultimately answer to stockholders, employees of mutual insurance companies work directly for the policyholders.

In stockholder-owned companies, the board of directors must act in the best interest of those stockholders. The stockholders—not the policyholders—participate in the company's profits.

Mutual insurance companies collect policy premiums, just as publicly traded insurers do. Each year, a portion of those revenues are reserved for what the company is likely to pay out in the form of death benefits. Another portion of revenues goes to cover salaries and various expenses.

Insurers typically have a surplus after funds are set aside for death benefits and operating expenses. It's important to remember that the insurance company is legally required to set aside reserves to cover anticipated obligations. Due to the conservative nature of the company structure, it is often the case that more funds are set aside than expenses paid out during the year.

In a mutual insurance company, directors decide once a year whether dividends are to be paid from the surplus reserves. While there is no guarantee that policyholders will receive dividends, a large majority of mutual insurance companies, for more than 100 years, have paid dividends.

Your dividend can be used to repay loans, or it can go toward your policy's cash value. The dividend can be paid directly to you in cash. It can also be used to buy additional insurance through what are known as paid up additions (more on them shortly). The choice is yours. By the way, corporate dividends are subject to taxes, but this may not be the case with dividends from mutual insurers.

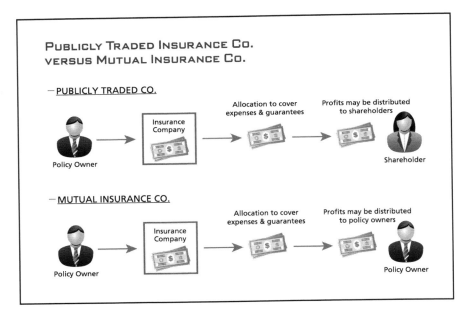

Now we will compare a "conventional" whole life policy with one that is custom-designed for use as your Private Vault. Normally, the main focus of whole life policies is solely to provide a death benefit. That's why they're also referred to as "permanent" policies—they are life insurance that remains in force throughout your entire life. Policyholders can't "lose" the way they can with term policies, because a death benefit will be paid no matter when they die.

Along with the death benefit, whole life policies include a cash-value component. This cash account within the insurance is funded by your premiums, and it accrues a guaranteed minimum rate of interest throughout the life of the policy.

Now, building up this cash reserve is not the first goal of *conventional* permanent policies. The immediate goals, once again, are to provide life insurance and to "force" us to save money in a disciplined way. As a result, it can take up to 15 years for a policy's cash value to equal the total of our premium payments.

As our cash value grows, it does so tax-free until the amount of dividends exceed the premiums we have paid. (If this does occur, it's wise to allocate the dividend payments to the purchase of what are known as paid-up additions, which we'll discuss in a moment. Another alternative to allowing dividend payments to accumulate in the policy's cash-value account is to allocate them to pay premiums or pay outstanding loans.) Provided that the dividends have not exceeded the premiums paid, the growth is not subject to taxation unless the policy is surrendered or withdrawals exceed the amount of premiums paid.

Conventional whole life policies are not designed as a financing vehicle—in other words, they're not designed as Private Vaults. However, your insurance agent has the ability to tailor permanent policies for just this purpose.

Using "Riders" to Customize a Mutual Whole Life Policy

The main way that policies are customized is through the use of policy additions, also known as riders. Let's look at three key types of riders.

✓ **Paid-up additions**. "PUAs" are a way to buy additional insurance within your original policy. Using them to pay more toward your policy results in an increased death benefit, higher cash value, and potentially greater dividends. Most importantly for your private banking plan, paid-up PUAs let you increase the amount of money you're stuffing into your policy. That increase comes in two ways—in the form of the portion of your premium that's applied to your cash value and in the form of dividend payments that can also be applied to your cash value. The result is a multiplier effect that causes the cash value to grow quickly.

- Understanding how paid-up additions compound the growth in your policy is very important. Here's an example: Frank originally had a policy with a death benefit of $100,000. When the board of directors of the insurance company declares a dividend payment to the policyholders, the payments are usually allocated to each policyholder based on the amount the policyholder has contributed to the surplus. Over the past several years, Frank has paid additional premium payments and directed his annual dividend to be used to purchase paid-up additions. Before long, Frank's death benefit has increased to $200,000, and he now participates in twice the dividend payment he did when his death benefit was $100,000.

✓ **Guaranteed Insurability Rider**. As the name suggests, this rider ensures your eligibility for insurance for the future. That means you'll be able to add paid-up additions as long as you wish.

✓ **Waiver of Premium Rider**. This rider ensures that your policy premiums will continue to be paid even if disability leaves you unable to make payments on your own.

Indexed Universal Life Insurance

In designing your Private Vault, you have the option to use a type of permanent insurance known as indexed universal life (IUL). IUL policies (IULs) allow you to participate in index appreciation without exposing you to market dips.

In IULs, funds earmarked for the policy's cash-value component are allocated to two accounts. The first is an account that is guaranteed to generate a set rate of interest. In the second account, growth is linked to the performance of a market index.

The index account allows you to capture a portion of the market's performance—in other words, it allows you to potentially surpass the interest rate in your first account. At the same time, policyholders are contractually protected against loss.

- Remember Mary's dilemma? She purchased a term policy and paid $50,000 in premiums over 10 years. When the 10-year term period expired, she had nothing to show for all her payments. And unfortunately, if she had invested that $50,000 directly in the S&P 500, she would have lost 9%—leaving her with only $45,500 after 10 years. However, suppose Mary had purchased an IUL policy and allocated her $50,000 to the index account, and linked the account to the S&P 500 index. In that case, after the same 10-year period, the account would have grown 8%, to $118,368. Additionally, since IUL is permanent insurance, Mary's policy would still be full force after the 10-year period.

It is possible to avoid losses even in the worst markets because, while your cash is linked to an index, it is not literally invested in the market. The insurer applies market gains to your account, but it does nothing when the market falls. The bottom line: IULs provide policyholders with a "floor" that keeps them from losing money. Some insurance companies will even set the "floor" at 1% or 2% annually—thus guaranteeing that the account will continue to grow even if the underlying index declines in value. (As we will see in later chapters, when the insurance company sets a floor above zero, our upside growth may be limited in the policy.)

7

Structuring
the Private Vault

N ow we can start to think about how to structure and use
life insurance to serve as our Private Vault. We know
we should use a permanent life policy from a mutual insurer
so that dividends are paid to us as the policyholder. Let's take
a moment to understand how dividends are paid.

First of all, unlike the dividends you might earn by investing in a company on the stock exchange, the dividends paid
by your insurance company may not be subject to taxes. Allocated into your cash account, they provide compounding,
tax-free growth until the amount of accumulated dividend
exceeds the premiums paid into the policy.

It's important to know that your policy's cash value enjoys
legal protection. Most states do not permit judgments allowing creditors to have access to that cash, although each state
sets its own level of protection. For example, residents of
Florida have their entire cash value protected from creditors
under the Florida statutes. See Appendix B.

Loans from Your Policy

lity to borrow from your policy is what makes it your
Priv. Vault. When you take a loan through your insurance,
you are not only bypassing the bank, but you are *borrowing
against a cash value that will continue to accumulate.*

Because you'll be receiving dividend payments and taking
loans, it's important to note that the amount of dividend you
receive while you are borrowing money will vary based on the
type of insurance company behind your policy.

Specifically, you'll want to use what's known as a "non-
direct recognition" mutual insurance company. This particular
kind of company pays policyholders the same level of dividend
regardless of whether they have a loan outstanding or not.

On the other hand, "direct-recognition" companies pay
higher dividends for those without outstanding loans. They
put borrowers at a disadvantage when it comes to dividend
payments.

Overpaying on Purpose

As we've discussed, the concept of Economic Value Added
teaches us that our money has a potential value beyond just
making purchases. Our Private Vault strategy allows us to
gain the largest lifelong benefit that our money can provide.
The key is to make larger premium payments than we are
required to make.

Those overpayments let us acquire paid-up additions to
our policies—and those PUAs can kick the growth of our
cash value into a higher gear. Not only do they directly grow
our cash value, but they serve to boost the dividends going

into that cash account. Dividends are based upon a policy-holder's death benefit: The more paid-up additions you add to your policy, the greater your death benefit—and thus your dividends—will be.

- Remember the case of Frank in the last chapter, Chapter 7, "Understanding Insurance Options"? Frank purchased PUAs by paying excess premiums and dividends. The PUAs increased the value of Frank's death benefit and thus increased the amount of dividends allocated to his policy. The same result would have occurred if Frank had taken a loan and paid more than the minimum amount due in repayments. The additional loan payments can be used for PUAs.

Please note that paid-up additions only apply to whole life policies. It's possible to make payments in an indexed universal life policy that exceed required premium or loan repayments. In that case, the additional payments will increase your cash accumulation value and thus provide greater funds to either generate guaranteed interest or to be invested in an index-linked account within the IUL policy. More about IULs shortly.

Withdrawing Funds versus Taking Loans

It's possible to withdraw cash from your policy, rather than taking loans against the value of the policy. It's part of the flexibility that isn't available in a 401(k) or IRA. For example, if you need to withdraw funds from a retirement account, you will pay tax at your personal tax bracket and may be subject to a 10% early withdrawal penalty. However, making withdrawals rather than taking loans from your policy carries a cost.

When you withdraw money from your policy, interest stops accruing. Furthermore, if you withdraw a total that is greater than the premiums you have paid, your money may be subject to taxes.

Contrast that with taking a loan. When you borrow from a policy rather than withdrawing funds, the cash in the policy continues to accrue interest. That's because you are not borrowing your cash directly—your insurance company uses your cash as collateral for a loan that it makes to you. Furthermore, when you take a withdrawal from the policy, you reduce the size of your policy. The withdrawal is permanent and the funds from the withdrawal cannot be put back into your policy later on. This result is very different from a loan, which is intended to be paid back into the policy.

It's critical to keep a long-term perspective about the goal of your insurance policy. The aim is to increase the policy's cash value over time, not deplete it through hasty withdrawals. The Private Vault is not a get-rich-quick scheme.

With patience, you will be able to break your dependence on banks and lenders and become financially independent. You'll be able to do whatever borrowing you require from your own, private bank. This process doesn't happen in one fell swoop, but rather little by little.

By remaining disciplined, you'll get closer each year to financial independence. In controlling your own debt—rather than having the corner bank control it—you'll build your wealth faster. Amazingly, the greatest impact on your wealth will come from eliminating your need for banks and other lenders.

It can't be stated enough that patience and discipline are essential to the success of the Private Vault strategy. You must treat it as a savings vehicle, not an ATM. You must overpay premiums to the greatest extent possible in order to increase your death benefit through PUAs, and thus your stream of dividend income. The faster you build your cash value, the faster you will be able to refinance bank debt with "Private Vault debt." The sooner you stop banks from siphoning off your wealth, the sooner you can start accumulating it for yourself and your family.

Being Your Own Lender

Let's review exactly what you gain by borrowing from yourself rather than borrowing from a bank or using your savings to make a purchase. When you borrow from a bank, the bank calls all the shots. It sets the interest rate, the origination fees, and the repayment schedule. Your role? It's as simple as signing on the dotted line.

When you save money to make purchases, you lose the opportunity to use that money to your benefit in other ways—that's the opportunity cost. Because you need your cash to be readily available for the purchase, you keep it in a low-yielding account, where you may be lucky just to keep up with inflation.

Borrowing against your insurance policy enables you to avoid all of these drawbacks. First of all, the loan qualification process is extremely simple and fast: Policyholders can access up to two-thirds of their cash value almost immediately by letting the insurance company know they want a loan.

The opportunity-cost issue is eliminated because your money remains in your account generating a return. Remember, you are not dipping into your own cash for loans; the insurance company is extending the loan and simply using your cash balance as collateral.

By the way, borrowing against insurance is superior to borrowing from your 401(k) or other qualified retirement plan. When you borrow from your retirement account, you are required to repay the funds within five years (unless for the purchase of a primary residence). Just as money withdrawn from your savings account can no longer earn bank interest, money borrowed from your 401(k) can't grow with market appreciation. What's more, the consequences of being late on a 401(k) loan payment are costly: The outstanding loan balance is treated as a taxable distribution from the date of the missed payment. To make matters worse, if you're younger than 59½, you may face a 10% early withdrawal penalty.

Because it's so easy to borrow from your whole life policy, it's critical that you exercise financial discipline. Although you are borrowing from your policy, you must treat the transaction as though you were borrowing from a bank. You must be committed to repaying the loan. The only exception is if you are financing your retirement, which we will discuss shortly.

Remember, we want our cash reserves to compound. We do that by faithfully repaying the loan—along with additional interest. That extra interest bolsters the compounding of our cash reserves because it buys us paid-up additions. Those PUAs increase our death benefit, and consequently the dividends that are based upon that death benefit and paid into our cash accounts.

Again, the reason for paying more interest than necessary in a whole life policy is strictly to buy paid-up additions, which leads to faster growth of our cash.

Evaluating Whole Life Policies

Every insurance product has strengths and weaknesses, and it's important to understand them before committing to that product. Let's look at participating whole life policies first; we'll explore indexed universal life policies in the next chapter.

One of the key strengths of a whole life policy is that it provides a death benefit immediately. Your loved ones have a financial cushion in the event of your death. That death benefit can be increased over time through the use of paid-up additions.

Whole life policies obtained through a mutual insurance company can pay a consistent dividend. And their predictable rate of return provides certainty that allows us to make financial plans with confidence. What's more, even when we have an outstanding loan against our policy, the funds within that policy continue to grow and compound.

Whole life policies also provide tax-free growth. Our country's tax code favors the preservation of wealth rather than the generation of wealth. Wealthy people understand this and use these financial vehicles to protect their wealth. You should too.

Finally, whole life insurance allows you to make purchases that you would have made anyway. By using policy loans, you have the ability to pay yourself back, rather than the bank.

Now for the weaknesses. First and foremost, you must be insurable in order to participate, as with any insurance product. Second, whole life policies are not designed to generate immediate wealth—they provide the advantage of consistent returns over time.

For the purposes of creating your private banking system, permanent policies must be customized. You can't use an off-the-shelf version to create your Private Vault.

Your plan must be specially designed so that it is not funded too rapidly. In 1988, tax law was changed to address the practice of people stuffing big chunks of wealth into whole life policies. The government considered this an obvious ploy to simply avoid taxes, which it usually was. Under current law, funding must be spread out properly in order to avoid taxes and stiff penalties. This is known as the Seven-Pay Test. If a policy fails to meet the Seven-Pay Test, or if there is not a sufficient corridor between the cash value and the amount of death benefit, the policy will become a Modified Endowment Contract (MEC).

- You want to structure your policy to avoid it being an MEC. If your policy is considered an MEC, any amounts that you borrow based upon the gain inside of the policy will be treated as taxable to you. This is known as last-in first out (LIFO). Additionally, if you withdraw funds prior to age 59½, you will incur a 10% penalty.

It's also important to understand when to take loans and when to take withdrawals. Depleting your capital through withdrawals can jeopardize your long-term plan to achieve financial independence. Likewise, you must understand when and how to repay the loans you take against your policy.

A final word of caution about whole life is that it's not for thrill seekers. Whole life policies' cash accounts don't participate in market upswings (IULs can, as we'll discuss in the next chapter). They won't give you much to brag about when talk at the golf club turns to stock picking. They are for those of us who value the slow, consistent growth of our capital without risk of loss.

8

Understanding
Indexed Universal Life

Indexed universal life insurance is what's known as investment-grade life insurance, but I find this terminology misleading. "Investment" implies the risk of losing money, and that risk doesn't exist with indexed universal life.

IULs are designed to capture market appreciation while eliminating downside risk for the policyholder. To quickly review how these policies work: IULs allow for flexible premium payments. A portion of the IUL premium is allocated to an annual renewable term policy. The remaining portion of the premiums is allocated between two cash-value accounts— an interest-bearing account that generates a guaranteed rate of return, and an account that tracks a market index. Policyholders can add additional premium payments—subject to IRS tax guidelines—and the additional funds go to increase the value of the cash accounts.

IUL policyholders enjoy the flexibility of allocating funds between the accounts as they wish on an annual basis. A portion of their capital can generate a guaranteed rate of return (the interest-bearing account), and a portion can participate in market growth based upon underlying linked indexes (the indexed account). The policyholder can allocate all of the funds to one account or the other.

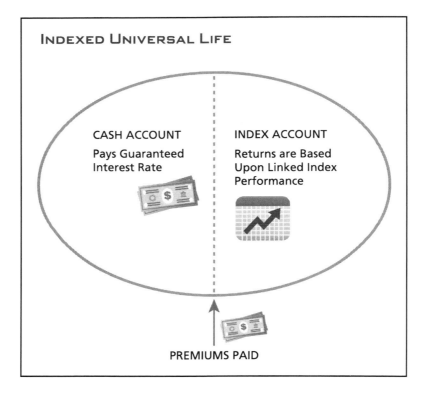

If John believes that for the next year the market is going to be on a steady downturn, he may elect to have all of the capital set aside in his interest-bearing account. By shifting the capital to the interest-bearing account, John ensures that the account will continue to receive a guaranteed return even if the market declines in value.

Conversely, if John believes that the market is going to end up with a higher return than the guaranteed value in the interest-bearing account, he may transfer all of the capital to the index account. If the underlying index increases 10% that year, his account will grow in value based upon the positive returns. The best thing is that if John is wrong and the underlying index drops 10%, he doesn't lose any of his account value. John's worst-case scenario is that his account will remain even. Can you say that about your 401(k)?

A key feature of IULs has to do with the ability to set your level of participation in the market's performance. This is where we get into the terminology of "cap," "participation rate," and "floor." The cap is simply the percentage of the market's growth that you capture. If the policy has a cap rate of 13% and the S&P 500 increases 15%, you are capped at 13% growth. The participation rate is the amount of return you will receive within your policy cap rate. I recommend using policies that have a 100% participation rate. Looking at the example above, your account would receive 100% of the 13% growth. If your policy has a 75% participation rate, you'll participate in 75% of the of the 13% growth. Some companies even provide participation rates in excess of 100% for a set number of years within the life of the policies.

You may be wondering why a cap rate exists at all. Cap rates exist because insurance companies allocate funds to purchase options from banks on the underlying indexes. The options that the companies purchase have the cap rates built into the option contract. The higher the cap rate, the more expensive the option contract.

The floor, on the other hand, is the maximum percentage you can lose. The floor is a truly nifty feature of IULs— because all policies will have a 0% floor. In other words, no matter how much the index falls, you won't lose any capital. Some policies are even structured to have a floor of 1% or 2%: Even if the index falls, you are guaranteed a positive return. There is a tradeoff, however. Insurers who provide floors of more than 0% typically limit either their cap or participation rate in some manner.

It's important to understand that the cash value within the index account is not used to directly buy shares in the market. The account receives a return based on the index that it tracks. The most common indexes that are used are the S&P 500, Russell 2000, Barclays Capital U.S. Aggregate Bond Index, and EURO STOXX 50. Instead of purchasing the S&P 500 outright, the insurance company buys what are known as option contracts on that index in order to allow policyholders to participate in its appreciation but not its losses.

An option is a contract that gives you a right to purchase an asset for a predetermined price in the future. Since the price is locked, you pay a fee for the option contract. Imagine that you want to buy a home for $250,000, but you are unsure if the real estate market has stabilized, and you don't want to lose money on the purchase. You buy an option from the seller for $10,000 to buy the home one year from now for $250,000. In a year's time, when the value of the home is $275,000 you will exercise your option to purchase the property for $250,000, which is now below market value. If in a year the value of the home decreases to $225,000, you will not exercise the option because you would be paying $250,000 for a property that is only worth $225,000 one year later. By not exercising the option, you lose the $10,000 that you paid for the option contract but you are not forced to be upside down on the purchase of the home.

Two accounts within an IUL policy means that policyholders have a choice when it comes to borrowing against their cash value. Let's say the interest rate on your loan will be 3%. And let's say your fixed-return account is generating 3%. If you borrow from that account, it's a wash—the interest rate you pay cancels out the return you are earning.

On the other hand, you can have the interest rate set at a variable rate, and you have the opportunity to come out ahead. When loans are taken out of the policy and the interest is paid at a variable rate, the insurance company will treat the principal as still inside of the policy and it will be able to participate in the index gains. If the index jumps 11% over the life of your loan, and you're paying a variable rate of 5.2%, you're up 5.8 percentage points. On the other hand, if your index account returns 0%, you're still paying the variable rate. It is important to understand the rate of the variable loan. Many companies currently charge 5.5% on the variable rates. Many companies will limit the future rate of the variable loan in order to make lending an attractive option even in the case of future high inflation.

Lock and Reset

Another attractive feature of indexed universal life is known as "lock and reset." Lock and reset complements the "floor" feature by ensuring that we aren't affected by market loss. First the lock feature: At the end of each year, the cash in your account is "locked." Let's say it's the end of the year and you've participated in a market gain. That gain is locked in as principal and it's immune to any future loss. Now suppose that it's the end of a year in which the market index that your policy is linked to has declined by 20%. Because you have a 0% "floor," you haven't lost money.

Even better, because of your policy's "reset" feature, you don't have to wait for the index to make up that 20% decline before you can participate in new gains. The reset feature makes the index's level at the beginning of the new year your starting point. You participate in any gains in this new year, up to your cap.

Claire's policy is a good illustration of the lock and reset feature. She has her indexed account linked to the S&P 500.

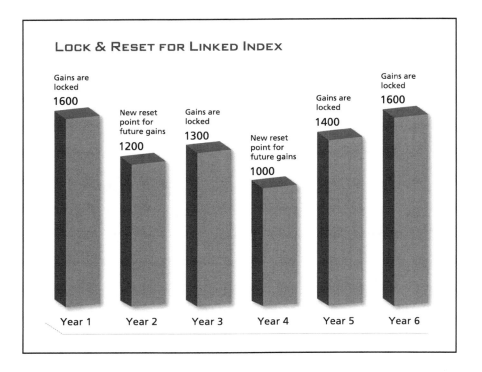

LOCK & RESET FOR LINKED INDEX

Gains are locked
1600
Year 1

New reset point for future gains
1200
Year 2

Gains are locked
1300
Year 3

New reset point for future gains
1000
Year 4

Gains are locked
1400
Year 5

Gains are locked
1600
Year 6

When Claire purchased her policy, the S&P 500 index was at 1,400. On her anniversary date, the S&P 500 was up 10%, to 1,540. Since Claire's policy had a cap rate of 13% and 100% participation, her account increased in value the full 10%. The next year the S&P 500 was down 20%, to 1,232. If Claire had been directly invested in the S&P 500, her account would have lost 20%.

Thankfully, Claire was not directly invested the S&P 500. Her policy doesn't directly participate in the market, and because of its floor, she did not lose money. The new value of S&P 500 at 1,232 becomes Claire's new floor. She doesn't have to wait for the S&P 500 to claw back to 1,400 to break even; Claire will participate in the growth each year as the S&P 500 goes back up. At the end of each year a new lock and reset occurs protecting her against any loss.

There is a huge difference in your capital's exposure within an IUL policy as compared with investing directly in the market. When you invest in the stock market in the usual way, it's as though you're sailing on the open sea. With an IUL policy, you're in a safe port. Now consider what the weather is like on the open seas.

Historically, the United States has experienced a recession or a market correction every eight years, as Terry Laxton notes in his book, *The Better Money Method*. On average, the market takes 18 months to recover from its low point. In other words, you as an investor spend a year and a half just getting back to even—and that's if you stay fully invested. Remember, many investors panic and sell their investments in a market correction, which only locks in losses.

On the other hand, if you have your capital in an IUL policy with a floor, you can start making money again while other investors are struggling simply to get back to the starting line. You have a huge head start in the capital-appreciation race.

Strengths and Weaknesses of IULs

Let us review by evaluating the strengths and weaknesses of indexed universal life insurance:

Strengths

- ✓ IULs allow us to participate in market growth *and* earn a guaranteed rate of return.

- ✓ Thanks to their "floor" feature, we cannot lose money in the market.

✓ Their annual "reset" feature protects us from having to recover market losses.

✓ IUL premiums are typically lower than those of conventional whole life policies.

✓ IULs allow for flexible premiums.

Weaknesses

✓ Market participation can potentially yield 0% growth.

✓ Having funds in an index-linked account removes the predictability of returns that you have in a regular whole life policy from a mutual insurance company.

✓ Your IUL policy could get more expensive annually if it's built around a term-life policy.

9

Taking Control and Implementing a Lifelong Plan

B enjamin Franklin famously said that time is money. When it comes to setting up and funding your Private Vault, that is literally true. It's important to create our customized policies as soon as we can: The sooner we do so, the closer we are to financial independence, and the longer we'll be able to take advantage of it. Waiting just a few years can have a tremendous impact on the value of your Private Vault. Here's an example:

- Bob is 43 years old and is weighing the pros and cons of purchasing an IUL policy now or waiting until he's 48. Bob can easily afford a $12,000 annual premium and he wants to have $1 million in initial insurance coverage.

- If Bob takes out his policy at age 43 and pays $12,000 a year into the plan, at age 53 he should have accumulated $125,000 in capital in his vault. If Bob waits until age 48 to start, and pays the same $12,000 annual premium, at age 53 his Private Vault would be worth just $17,000. Waiting five years to start the policy would create a gap in accumulated capital of $103,000—despite a difference in the amount of premium paid of only $60,000.

- The outcome of starting later becomes more pronounced with time. If Bob starts his policy at age 43, then by the time he is 66 (and has stopped paying premiums) the cash in his Private Vault will have grown to $551,000. At that point, Bob will be able to begin drawing off the account in the form of income-tax–free loans that will supplement his retirement for the remainder of his life. What's more, the death benefit that will pass to his family will have increased to $1,551,000. If, on the other hand, Bob waits until age 48 to start his policy, the cash value in his Private Vault will have grown to just $261,000 by the time he reaches age 66. Now, this amount is still respectable considering that Bob's capital has not been subject to loss and has been used to finance purchases. But its value is still more than 50% less than it would have been if Bob had started the policy a mere five years earlier.

A question I'm commonly asked is whether it makes sense to set up a Private Vault if you're already at retirement age or older. The answer is often yes. If you're older, you won't necessarily reap the benefit of decades of growth on your money. However, you *will* begin to benefit immediately from consistent, predictable growth, as opposed to investing in the stock market and hoping for growth.

Furthermore, you will have the added advantage of a death benefit to bestow upon your family. Remember, that death benefit takes effect right from the time you make your first premium payment.

Your Lifetime and Beyond

Permanent life insurance in general, and a customized policy in particular, allows us to create a financial strategy that extends beyond the lifetime of ourselves and our spouses. One way to implement this multi-generational strategy is to name children, grandchildren, or nieces and nephews as beneficiaries of the policies.

A more direct way to do it, and a way that holds the potential for more involvement and education of your younger family members, is to set up and fund policies either in their names or with you as the owner of the policy. This is perfectly legal as long as you have what's known as an "insurable interest" in the insured person. You have an insurable interest in someone when his or her injury or death would cause you to suffer a financial loss or other kind of loss.

Both of these ownership approaches have merit. It is the owner of the policy who has the ability to access the cash accumulation of the policy. If a parent or grandparent names a child or grandchild as the owner of the policy, the child or grandchild has the ability to directly borrow from his or her own Private Vault to pay for education, vehicles, real estate, and so on.

If the parent or grandparent is the owner of the policy, the funds can still be loaned out to cover education expenses, and the policy can be used as a lending source for the child or grandchild. The biggest advantage of this approach is that it allows the parents or grandparents who own the policy to access the Private Vault for their own needs as well as those of their loved ones.

Decisions about policy ownership often play out in two common scenarios:

- **Scenario 1**: As grandparents, David and Melanie want to provide a lifetime funding strategy to cover their grandchildren's expenses. Additionally, the couple wants to supplement their own retirement. Thus far, the grandchildren haven't demonstrated the best money management skills, and David and Melanie are concerned that if a grandchild is the owner of the policy, that grandchild could completely cash out the policy at age 18. In order to prevent this from happening and to supplement their own retirement income, the couple decides to take out a policy on each of their grandchildren.

  As their grandchildren grow, they will have the funds to help cover education costs. Loans taken to cover college expenses will be paid back over time. When David and Melanie are ready to retire, they will have created a tax-free, retirement-income source for themselves even as they have helped finance their grandchildren's needs as well.

- **Scenario 2**: Denny and Betty are nearing retirement and have financially responsible grandchildren. Denny and Betty do not need any additional income for their retirement, but they do want to help with their grandchildren's future education expenses. Denny and Betty know their grandchildren would not consider cashing out the policies at age 18, so they're comfortable designating the grandchildren as the owners of their policies at age 18.

  Denny and Betty will gift an amount each year to cover the policies' premium payments. The grandchildren will now have their very own Private Vaults from which to borrow funds to cover education costs, vehicle purchases, down payments on homes, and, after many years of asset growth, retirement.

Within the mainstream financial industry, you might hear that there's no point in taking out a permanent life insurance policy on a child. And it's true enough that kids don't usually have dependents whom they need to protect with a death benefit. But this rationale overlooks a major planning opportunity: Permanent life insurance can be used as a wealth-building strategy that can benefit the policyholder throughout his or her life.

A properly designed policy can be the basis of a family dynasty of consistent tax-free growth and access to financing. It can be used as a family financial tool in the near term and to create a legacy for future generations. Think about the typical pattern of how we save. Most of us only get serious about saving money for retirement and other long-term goals in our 30s, or even in our 40s.

Let's say, on the other hand, that you start a policy on a 10-year-old child. By the time that child has retired, he will have had 55 years of compound growth in his policy.

Remember that you can use either a dividend-paying whole life policy, or, if you'd like the child to participate in market upswings without any risk of loss to principal, an indexed universal life policy.

During the child's lifetime the money in his or her policy will be safe from capital loss and exorbitant fees. What's more, its cash value will be available throughout the child's life to fund everything from car purchases to college.

The Private Vault strategy is a great way to teach children and grandchildren about financial independence even as we help them to achieve it.

Redirection of Payments

Now let's look more closely at specific ways that using your permanent life policy as your Private Vault can benefit you. I'm going to use an example most of us can relate to: buying a car.

When we buy a car, we typically finance it, taking out a loan from a bank to pay the car dealer. Month in and month out, our car-loan payments are directed to the bank. In short, we're giving away money to someone else.

What if we were to redirect that payment to ourselves? In his fine book, *The Banking Effect*, Dan Thompson explains that by diverting debt payments from third-party lenders and rerouting it to the *bank of you*, you can end up with savings that are equivalent to enormous investment returns.

Many families look at their debt payments and their investment returns as separate issues; they're resigned to making debt payments, and they hope that their investments do well. Successful, wealthy people don't see things this way. They understand that debt and income are related within the larger context of their family balance sheets.

The ratio of household income to debt payments can easily be 35%: If we earn $100,000 a year, we pay a staggering $35,000 in debt. A typical family, if they are diligent, might save 5% of their income each year—$5,000. Remember: $35,000 in annual debt payment compared with $5,000 in savings. It's quite a mismatch.

Just out of curiosity, how much would we have to earn on our savings to neutralize the $35,000 we use to service debt? About 700% per year, Thompson explains. Even if we invest our savings in the strongest bull market ever, we'll never be able to compensate for the money we give away in the form of debt payments. If we're lucky, maybe we'll earn 10% in a given year on that $5,000 savings, giving us a $500 profit.

Look at what happens when we redirect even a small percentage of the money we give away in the form of debt payments back to ourselves. Let's redirect that car payment. A typical car payment is around $250 a month, which works out to $3,000 a year. Suppose that instead of using a bank loan to pay for the car, we take a loan against the cash balance in our permanent life policy.

All of a sudden, we are not just giving away those monthly payments to a bank—we're effectively repaying ourselves. In a very real sense, we are saving that $3,000 each year. Ben Franklin's maxim, "A penny saved is a penny earned," is absolutely true—the man understood that it's all about the overall balance sheet!

Now think about what kind of return we'd have to earn on our $5,000 of savings in order to earn $3,000. Our money would have to generate returns of 60%. If you find an investment that pays 60% every year, please let me know!

Remember, we reach our financial goals not just by bringing money in but by giving less of it away. Using that balance-sheet perspective, we can see that redirecting those car payments to our Private Vault is the equivalent of earning a 60% return on our money.

Through the use of our private bank, we have substantially outperformed any savings or investment account. Furthermore, we've done so *without any risk*. No investment in existence can claim that. Does that help to give you an idea of the power of your Private Vault?

Now let's extrapolate. Suppose the $3,000 car payment is just a fraction of your annual debt payments, which is very likely. A family with $100,000 of annual income might easily pay out $15,700 a year, and that's not even including mortgage payments.

The more of that debt payment you can direct to your Private Vault, the greater your equivalent return will be. The numbers start to become staggering: If a family transferred all of their $15,700 in annual debt payments to their private bank, they'd earn an equivalent return of about 200%. It should be clear by now that transferring your debt from third-party lenders such as banks to your Private Vault is a powerful way to grow your wealth.

You may not be able to transfer all your debt into your private banking system right away. But as you build your cash value, you will gradually be able to take charge of your financial life and become financially independent.

What's more, the more you borrow against your policy, the more you can boost your returns. Specifically, in making loan payments, you can opt to pay excess interest; that interest buys you paid-up additions in a whole life policy or additional cash contributions in an IUL policy.

Financing Purchases

Since you already know that your Private Vault can be used to finance major purchases, it's time to take a look at how the process will play out in real life.

Let's use the hypothetical example of purchasing a car. We'll name the couple in our example Ross and Elaine. Ross, 32, commutes 40 minutes each day to his job in the tech industry. He needs a dependable car that's comfortable enough for the long back-and-forth twice a day. Elaine, 26, is an interior-decorating consultant. She wants a safe, reliable automobile that also makes a good impression on her clients.

Ross and Elaine have been discussing their personal and professional plans with their insurance specialist. They plan to start a family, but not just yet. With their careers going well, they want to make sure they lay a strong foundation for managing their money and making sure it translates into reaching their long-term goals.

Their insurance specialist, John, advises the couple to consider using mutual whole life insurance as a long-term savings and investment vehicle. With a policy specifically designed for their needs, Ross and Elaine will be able to count on a liquid, tax-advantaged savings pool with a predictable rate of return, he explains.

They'll also be able to bequeath a substantial death benefit to their future children. Finally, they'll have the ability to finance the purchase of cars, real estate, and other major items, when and how they wish to do so.

Ross and Elaine are intrigued by John's suggestion. They're convinced that a customized permanent life policy can provide a level of safety, predictability, and liquidity that conventional alternatives such as 401(k)s and IRAs can't match.

The couple's strategy will include using paid-up additions in order to grow their policy's cash value more quickly than they could through a basic whole life policy.

Working with John, they determine an annual premium payment that is substantial enough to grow their cash value relatively quickly, but leaves them a comfortable level of disposable income. Since Elaine is younger and healthier than Ross, the couple takes out the policy in her name.

Ross and Elaine have decided to reduce Elaine's 401(k) contributions and redirect these funds to her policy. After one year, Ross and Elaine have contributed $14,000 in premiums. After three years, thanks to the use of paid-up additions and consistent dividends, their cash value is significantly greater than it would be with a basic, "off-the-shelf" permanent life policy. The couple has access to two-thirds of the policy's accumulated cash value.

After three years, Elaine's car has started to spend a little too much time in the shop, and she decides it's time to buy that sleek new hybrid that she's had her eye on. The cash value in Elaine's policy has growth to $34,800. Elaine takes a loan of $29,500 against her policy.

Unlike with a bank loan, Elaine doesn't have to go through a lengthy qualification process, and she won't have to pay loan origination fees or service charges. Her insurance company doesn't need her credit score. In fact, Elaine isn't even required to disclose the purpose of the loan. She simply submits a one-page form requesting a loan of $29,500.

Within a couple of weeks, $29,500 has been wired into Elaine and Ross's bank account. The loan comes with a standard interest rate. And while Elaine can technically repay it whenever she wishes, she commits to making regular payments, just as she would with a bank. She understands that her insurer has lent her the money with her cash value as collateral, and that each time she makes a principal payment, the company's lien against her cash value is reduced by that amount. Remember, when you repay a bank loan, you simply send your money to the bank, never to see it again.

In fact, Ross and Elaine choose to make larger monthly payments on Elaine's car than they would make to a bank. Instead of paying $567 per month for five years, they plan to pay $600 per month. The overpayment amount serves to quickly increase the policy's cash value through the purchase of paid-up additions.

After five years, the car loan has been paid off. Over that period, the couple has paid $600 per month for a total of $36,000. That money has covered the policy premiums as well as the principal and interest on the car loan. It has also increased the policy's cash value, which now stands at $130,000. Part of the policy's growth is due to a design feature that directs dividends paid by the insurance company toward buying paid-up additions.

Had Elaine used a bank loan to buy her car, all she would have at this point would be a five-year-old car. She would have transferred $33,402 in principal, interest, and fees to the lender, depleting her wealth rather than growing it. When Ross decides a year later that he needs a new car, the couple take a loan from their policy without hesitation.

ELAINE'S WHOLE LIFE POLICY

$14,000 Annual Premium from Age 27 through 66

Age	Year	Contract Premium	Loan Amt. Less Div. To Pay Loan	Loan Payment	Loan Balance	Net Cash Value	Net Death Benefit
27	1	$14,000				$10,859	$668,919
28	2	$14,000				$22,674	$710,629
29	3	$14,000				$34,788	$751,323
30	4	$14,000	$29,500		$30,975	$16,747	$763,433
31	5	$14,000		$7,200	$25,369	$36,145	$814,314
32	6	$14,000		$7,200	$19,483	$56,727	$867,513
33	7	$14,000		$7,200	$13,303	$78,544	$922,955
34	8	$14,000		$7,200	$6,814	$101,122	$977,462
35	9	$14,000		$7,200	$0	$130,000	$1,031,163
36	10	$14,000				$148,533	$1,077,003
41	15	$14,000				$239,047	$1,291,605
47	21	$14,000				$399,743	$1,524,080
56	30	$14,000				$727,835	$2,070,773
66	40	$14,000				$1,060,709	$2,121,969

This is a hypothetical illustration and does not represent any specific policy from any carrier.

Indeed, Ross and Elaine will use their private bank to purchase cars throughout their lives using the built-in credit facility within their insurance policy. Throughout their lives, their insurer will pay a steady, predictable rate of return, even as Ross and Elaine dutifully repay their loans, even overpaying to the extent they can.

After 20 years, the couple will have bought and paid for several cars—and they'll have accrued a cash value of $371,000, along with a death benefit of $1,524,080. The couple know that their private bank is robust enough to help pay for their son Dashiell's fast approaching college expenses—and eventually to fund their retirement.

10

Paying for College

Now let's walk through an example of how an insurance policy might be used to help pay for a child's college education. This is where using your Private Vault can really get rewarding because it can help family members succeed in life.

Ben is completing his senior year of high school and in a few short months will be heading off to college. His parents, Tom and Elizabeth Smith, are prepared to help. In fact, they took out a permanent life policy on Ben when he was just seven years old.

They understood that the sooner they started, the more time their cash value would have to appreciate. Tom and Elizabeth appreciated that they could earn a consistent rate of return through a whole life policy, but because they wanted the opportunity to earn an even stronger return, they opted for an indexed universal life policy.

Remember, IULs allow the policyholder to capture market appreciation without the downside risk. Tom and Elizabeth's policy has a "cap" of 14% that allows them to participate in

100% of the first 14% of the underlying index appreciation. Additionally, the policy's guaranteed zero-percent "floor" prevents them from losing money when the market has a down year.

What's more, their IUL policy came with a "lock and reset" feature. The feature means that not only was the policy's cash value immune to market losses, but that fresh investment gains could start accruing each year no matter what level the market started at.

In the 11 years since Tom and Elizabeth set up the policy, the market had been up and down quite a bit. The couple's neighbor, Woody, recently complained that the assets in the 529 College Savings Plan he set up for his daughter were not much higher than they had been a decade earlier. Due to the cap, floor, and lock-and-reset features on Tom and Elizabeth's policy, they've seen a respectable return of 6%. Tom and Elizabeth have been diligent in funding the policy at $10,000 a year for the last 11 years. As such, the account balance has now grown to $150,000.

Tom and Elizabeth have agreed to borrow from the policy to finance Ben's college education, with the expectation that he will repay the loan over time.

Ben's college costs will be approximately $80,000 for four years. His parents can lend him $20,000 per year, or they can use student loans as part of the equation.

Since the cash value of the IUL policy is not considered an asset for financial aid purposes, Ben was able to qualify for assistance. Ben is eligible for $10,000 per year of student loans that are interest-free over the course of his four years of college. Rather than borrowing the entire $80,000 in college costs from his parents via their insurance policy, Ben can borrow half that amount from his parents and half in the form of student loans.

By borrowing less from the insurance policy, the Smith family will be able to defer repayment of principal and interest for four years. As a result, more cash will remain available within the policy should unexpected loan needs arise.

After Ben has completed college, his student loan payments will commence. Before the first payment is due, Ben's parents can take a loan against their policy to pay off the student loans in full. At this point, all $80,000 in education debt will have been transferred to Tom and Elizabeth's Private Vault.

This approach—temporarily using student loans and then repaying them quickly through an insurance-policy loan—has allowed the family to defer interest payments for four years on half of the loan amount.

Remember, funds in the IUL policy have continued to grow during Ben's college years. That's due to continuing premium payments and to loan repayments made by Ben's parents during his education.

What's more, Tom and Elizabeth have chosen to repay the loan at a higher interest rate than the insurance company required. The excess interest payments are added as additional premium, thus increasing the policy's cash value and death benefit.

Ben's parents don't need to make loan payments while their son is in college. Because of the flexible terms involved in borrowing from insurance, they could theoretically never repay the loans. However, under their agreement, Ben is committed to repaying the loans, just as he would repay conventional education loans.

What's more, in a properly designed and executed policy, Ben's parents won't be obligated to make premium payments while their son is in school. They can direct their insurer to apply their cash value toward their premium obligations.

The family has agreed that Ben will begin repaying the loan when he is situated in a well-paying job. If he graduates into the middle of a recession and can't find sufficient work for an extended period of time, he won't risk default as he would with a traditional student loan.

Ben and his parents have agreed on a reasonable repayment schedule, and within 10 years, he has repaid $80,000 of principal as well as the 3% interest rate that he and his parents agreed on at the time they began lending him money for college.

With Ben's college completed and paid for, Tom and Elizabeth must decide what to do with the policy, which has served its original purpose. They have two options. They can

SAVING FOR COLLEGE

Age 7 with $10,000 Annual Premium

Year	Age	Contract Premium	Loan	Loan Payment	Accumulative Value	Death Benefit
1	7	$10,000			$9,003	$1,009,003
11	17	$10,000			$156,055	$1,156,055
12	18		$10,000		$169,127	$1,158,702
13	19		$10,000		$183,327	$1,162,034
14	20		$10,000		$198,766	$1,166,143
15	21		$10,000		$215,552	$1,171,118
16	22		$40,000		$233,802	$1,145,779
17	23	$10,000		$10,000	$263,919	$1,182,580
18	24	$10,000		$10,000	$296,662	$1,222,291
19	25	$10,000		$10,000	$332,262	$1,265,155
20	26	$10,000		$10,000	$370,955	$1,311,421
21	27	$10,000		$10,000	$413,002	$1,361,363
22	28	$10,000		$10,000	$458,728	$1,415,320
23	29	$10,000		$10,000	$508,459	$1,473,630
24	30	$10,000		$10,000	$562,538	$1,536,654
25	31	$10,000		$10,000	$621,344	$1,604,785
26	32	$10,000		$10,000	$685,285	$1,706,376
27	33	$10,000		$10,000	$754,779	$1,886,498

This is a hypothetical illustration and does not represent any specific policy from any carrier.

transfer ownership of the policy to Ben, who will be able to use it for lifetime borrowing transactions and to fund his retirement.

Alternatively, Tom and Elizabeth can use the funds for their own retirement income—taking loans that they do not intend to or legally need to repay. They can arrange for the remaining cash value at the time of their death to be transferred to Ben or to his children, along with the policy's death benefit.

Another Scenario

Suppose that Tom and Elizabeth hadn't had the foresight or ability to take out that IUL policy while Ben was young. They may have taken out their own policy years later because they liked the general idea of achieving financial independence.

When Ben is 15, Tom and Elizabeth take a hard look at college costs and decide to use their existing policy to fund his education. They realize, however, that the cash value within their policy isn't adequate to cover $80,000 of loans. The couple's insurance expert explains that there are two ways to grow the policy's cash value quickly.

The couple can fund the policy "overtime" by putting as much of their income and savings as possible without destroying the policy's tax-favored status. Or they can accelerate cash value accumulation by cashing out of their retirement accounts and establishing a new policy. Even though they will be penalized for withdrawing their money early, the ability to help Ben with college, and the benefits of financial independence that their private bank can provide, convince Tom and Elizabeth to choose the second option. As in the first scenario, Ben agrees to repay his parents once he has completed college and has enough income to begin doing so.

Don't forget that the insurance policy that's been used to finance Ben's college education has a death benefit. What would happen if the owner of the policy—let's say it's Tom—passes away unexpectedly before Ben repays the loan? In that case, the loans and associated interest will be subtracted from the death benefit. The beneficiary, Elizabeth, will receive the death benefit minus the loan and interest amount. She and Ben would then discuss how and when he would repay the loan amount to her.

By using permanent insurance for college financing, the Smith family has benefited in several ways. They've obtained funding for Ben without having to go through an extensive qualification process. They've enjoyed the flexibility to repay the loans when and how they wish—which will take the pressure off their son if his first job doesn't pay much.

Furthermore, Ben will not send loan payments to a bank, never to be seen again. The money he repays will stay in the family. And it will have a huge impact on their future, either financing Tom and Elizabeth's retirement or serving as their son's private bank—and eventually financing *his* retirement. What kind of student loan from a bank can compete with *that*?

11

Financing Retirement

In each of the examples in our previous chapters, the folks who borrowed from their Private Vaults planned to repay their loans. You'll recall that Ross and Elaine bought cars using loans against the cash value in their whole life policy, and they repaid those loans just as they would if they had borrowed from a commercial bank. In the case of the Smith family, Ben agreed to repay the loans against his parents' IUL policy after he graduated and landed a good job.

But when it comes to financing retirement, loan repayment is typically not part of the plan. The idea is to take loans against your policy with no intent to repay them. Both participating whole life and IUL policies will allow you to do this. Let's run through a hypothetical example of how this works, using our automobile financers, Elaine and Ross.

Elaine and Ross's Retirement

Elaine and Ross started funding their policy when Ross was 32 and Elaine was 26. Although they paid the policy's premiums together, they took out the policy on Elaine, who was younger and healthier than Ross and thus easier and less expensive to insure.

The couple had opted for a participating whole life policy. They wanted financial certainty based upon consistent returns without the risk of market loss. Setting up a Private Vault was Elaine and Ross's cornerstone strategy for reaching their long-term financial goals. The pair enjoyed a liquid, tax-advantaged savings pool with a predictable rate of return, and they used it to finance automobiles.

In addition to purchasing their vehicles, Ross and Elaine also financed their son's education expenses using their Private Vault. As you recall, when the policy was being established, Elaine had decided to reduce her 401(k) contributions and direct those funds to pay the policy premiums. Ross and Elaine were diligent in repaying their earlier loans to help ensure that there would be funds to support them in their retirement years.

Their son Dashiell graduated from college when Ross was 56 and Elaine was 50. Ross has decided to retire from his tech company at age 67. Elaine will retire at the same time, when she's 61, and the couple has a lengthy bucket list that includes travel, cooking and language classes, gardening, and restoring classic cars.

As the couple's new life in retirement draws near, Dashiell is making the last few monthly loan repayments. Elaine and Ross have a cash balance of $953,905 in their policy, and they intend to use it to supplement their other investments to fund their golden years.

The couple plan to borrow $75,000 against the policy each year for 15 years to fund their retirement. They're factoring in Social Security, which will compliment their retirement income.

ELAINE'S WHOLE LIFE POLICY

Annual Loan of $75,000 to Fund Retirement

Age	Year	Contract Premium	Loan Amount	Net Cash Value	Net Death Benefit
27	1	$14,000		$10,859	$668,919
40	14	$14,000		$215,076	$1,250,476
50	24	$14,000		$451,866	$1,617,565
62	34	$0	$75,000	$918,408	$2,143,218
63	35	$0	$75,000	$880,789	$2,092,296
64	36	$0	$75,000	$840,901	$2,038,442
65	37	$0	$75,000	$798,814	$1,981,681
66	38	$0	$75,000	$754,395	$1,922,095
67	39	$0	$75,000	$707,517	$1,859,528
68	40	$0	$75,000	$658,011	$1,793,808
69	41	$0	$75,000	$605,730	$1,724,752
70	42	$0	$75,000	$550,510	$1,652,177
71	43	$0	$75,000	$492,097	$1,575,882
72	44	$0	$75,000	$430,274	$1,495,665
73	45	$0	$75,000	$364,844	$1,411,293
74	46	$0	$75,000	$295,595	$1,322,519
75	47	$0	$75,000	$222,270	$1,229,087
76	48	$0	$75,000	$144,642	$1,027,190

This is a hypothetical illustration and does not represent any specific policy from any carrier.

One of the exciting things about this approach is the tax savings compared to an alternative such as a 401(k). In borrowing $75,000 against their insurance policy, Elaine and Ross will pay no income taxes on that money. Why? Because it's a loan, not a distribution.

Suppose that the couple had taken $75,000 from their 401(k) accounts instead of borrowing it from their Private

Vault. Distributions from 401(k) plans are taxable, so assuming that Elaine and Ross are in a 30% tax bracket, they would have paid $22,500 in federal taxes. In other words, to get the $75,000 needed to finance a year of retirement from 401(k)s, they would have needed $107,000 [$75,000 + the tax figure].

When it comes to paying back those loans, well, Elaine and Ross won't. After they die, the insurance company will deduct the amount they owe from their death benefit and give what remains to their beneficiaries. In this case, the remaining death benefit will go to their son.

Elaine and Ross know that having benefited from the use of their policy as a tax-free source of income during retirement, they will be able to leave their excess death benefit as an additional value to their family wealth dynasty.

Tom and Elizabeth's Retirement

Tom and Elizabeth, you will remember, took out a policy on their son, Ben, when he was just 7 years old. Because their time horizon was fairly long and they wanted to participate in upside index gains without risk of loss, the couple chose an indexed universal life policy.

As planned, Tom and Elizabeth used their insurance policy to finance their son's college education to the tune of $80,000. As agreed, he has repaid his parents in principal and interest over the years. Remember that after the policy had served its original purpose in financing Ben's education, Tom and Elizabeth faced a choice.

They had to decide whether to transfer ownership of the policy to Ben, for his use as a private banking system, or to finance their own retirement income. They chose the latter.

Ben, having seen the wealth-building power of permanent insurance firsthand, decided to take out his own policy and follow in his parents' footsteps. When Tom and Elizabeth turn 70, they will take out a series of annual loans of $100,000 to finance their retirement for the next 20 years.

The couple and their insurance agent decide to structure their loan with a fixed interest rate. In such cases, the fixed interest rate is typically equal to the interest that would be generated within the cash portion of the account. Since the interest on Tom and Elizabeth's cash account is generating 3%, the insurance company structures the loan with a 3% interest rate, making it what's known as a "wash loan."

Although the wash-loan approach makes sense in Tom and Elizabeth's case, it does have a drawback. In wash loans, insurance companies will not treat the loaned amount as principal for future growth within the policy. In order for the loaned amount to be treated as still within the policy for growth purposes, the loan interest rate must be variable. Most companies will put a cap on how high the variable rate can be in the future.

Now, even though the couple plan to take the cash value in their account down to $1 million as a result of their loans, they will still be able to leave a death benefit of more than $1 million to their grandchildren.

The Late Starter

Thus far we've looked at case studies in which couples started funding insurance policies early in their adult lives. But what about an individual who is approaching retirement? Is it still possible to gain game-changing benefits from customized permanent life? The answer is yes.

Even if you're in your 60s or older and are just learning about how a "Private Vault" works, there's time to use your permanent insurance policy as a lending facility, as a tax-favored home for your money, and as a way to achieve financial independence and help your children to do so as well.

Let's use Glen as an example. Glen is 62, is in reasonably good health, and has $1,000,000 in stock market investments and savings—much of it through an inheritance. Glen is a widower, but he has two children to whom he would like to leave an inheritance if possible. However, Glen is already concerned about outliving his money. He needs to earn more than the 1% the bank is paying him on his savings, and he's wary of leaving a large amount in the stock market because of potential loss of principal. He needs a strategy that can generate greater returns without the potential loss of principal.

Glen lost his wife, Fran, two years ago, so he understands how quickly health circumstances can change. Parker, Glen's son, has mentioned that his friends Ross and Elaine use life insurance as a key element of their financial plan. Glen decides to get in touch with John, Ross and Elaine's insurance agent, to learn more.

John answers all of Glen's questions, explaining how a Private Vault strategy based on permanent insurance can indeed serve as an effective way to finance Glen's retirement and pass along wealth to his children.

Glen decides to move forward, buying an IUL policy that will be custom-designed by John. Glen has decided to allocate half of the funds he has in the stock market and savings to the IUL policy for the next five years. At the end of the five years, Glen has contributed $500,000 to the policy, and has an available cash value of $533,000. He also has a death benefit of $1.5 million available to his children, whom he has selected as his beneficiaries.

Within five years of starting the policy, Glen's cash value exceeds his total premium payments by $33,000. At this time, Glen starts taking Social Security payments. Although Glen had been eligible for Social Security income as early as age 62, he'd delayed taking it in order to receive larger annual payouts. Glen uses his annual Social Security income, which totals $22,000, to fund his policy for the next five years.

When Glen turns 72, his policy has a cash value of $728,000. Following a long-term plan designed with John, he is ready to take his first loan against the policy and cease premium payments. His annual loan of $50,000 is free from income tax, and it doesn't count as earned income for tax reporting purposes. Remember, taxes don't apply to Glen's principal or to the steady return that he's earned on it within his policy. Technically, the money in his account isn't being distributed to him—it's simply a loan, albeit one that Glen does not need to repay.

Glen's plan involves continuing to take loans against his policy throughout retirement. As he does, he and John will carefully monitor the impact of those loans on the policy's cash value. This will help to ensure that the policy continues to operate properly and to remain in force. Glen also remains mindful that the amount of outstanding loan will affect the policy's death benefit. If Glen passes away at age 90, he will have received $900,000 in retirement supplement from his policy loans, and the remaining death benefit of $499,000 will pass to his children. Not bad considering he only paid a total of $610,000 in premiums.

12

Financing
Investment Purchases

As an advisor, many of the clients I serve are real estate investors. They buy, fix up, and then sell real estate at a profit. It's often a lucrative and rewarding business. But even the most successful real estate entrepreneurs often face a quandary when it comes to financing.

Specifically, I'm talking about what are known as rehab loans. These are the loans given to real estate investors for purchasing homes that are in need of repairs. The investor borrows the money to buy and repair—or "rehab" the property—and then repays the loan once the property is sold, ideally for a profit. Generally, real estate investors can't go to a traditional bank to get rehab financing.

As a result, if you're a real estate investor, you must find other ways to come up with the cash. Theoretically it's possible to use the money in your bank account to finance a deal. Unfortunately, not too many of us have that kind of liquid cash at our disposal, especially if there are multiple rehabs occurring simultaneously. Another option is to arrange a private loan, from a family member, friend, or associate. Of course, only a minority of investors have the luxury of access to "private money." What's more, private loans can be perilous and too often lead to damaged relationships.

With bank loans out of the question, many real estate investors turn to specialized companies that provide short-term financing known as hard-money rehab loans. These "equity-based lending" companies typically provide loans based on the potential of the property that's to be bought and rehabbed. The loans are secured by the value of the real estate.

Hard-money lenders make loans available without factoring in borrowers' credit rating, income, or other typical underwriting factors. Not surprisingly, they typically charge premium interest rates.

As you have probably already guessed, real estate investing presents a perfect opportunity for using your Private Vault. By doing so, you can finance your own real estate investments, or you can function as a hard-money lender to other real estate investors.

Using your Private Vault to finance a real estate investment is simple. Remember, you don't need to jump through the qualification hoops that you'd face with a bank. You simply instruct your insurance company to send you a check for the desired amount.

The interest rate on your loan will likely be far lower than the typical hard-money rate. A hard-money lender might charge between 10% and 15% interest, whereas your insurance company's rate might be around 3% or 6%. Remember, for the purposes of growing your wealth within your private banking system, it's advantageous to pay more interest than is necessary.

Your nominal interest rate might be 5%. But if you repay the loan with, say 8% interest, that additional interest will be used for adding new paid-up additions if you are using a participating whole life policy. The more PUAs you add, the greater your death benefit, which translates into greater dividend income from your mutual insurer.

Your policy is designed to funnel dividend income into buying more PUAs, creating the multiplier effect that grows your cash value at a fast pace. As a result, not only can you earn a profit through real estate investing, but you can juice up the wealth creation within your Private Vault as well. If you are using an indexed universal life policy, the additional payments will increase your cash accumulation value and thus provide greater funds to either generate guaranteed interest or to be invested on the index side of the policy.

Hard-Money Lending

While my clients include real estate investors who rehab properties, they also include hard-money lenders. If you're a hard-money lender, you can use your savings to finance deals. Or you might be forced to keep assets held in cash for future loans—rather than having that cash deployed in a more profitable way. A better way to provide hard-money financing? Borrowing from your Private Vault.

Hard-money lenders who follow this approach should charge the typical higher interest rate for their loans. With ready access to capital for lending purposes, hard-money lenders will have no shortage of eager investors looking for capital. To structure the transaction, the hard-money lender and the investor will enter into a contract for the amount of the loan. In order to properly secure your position, you—the hard-money lender—will secure a deed of trust (lien) against the property to protect your equity position. If the investor fails to repay the loan, you can foreclose on the property and either sell it to recover your equity, or add the property to your investment portfolio. Using a Private Vault creates a win–win situation for hard-money lenders.

By paying back your private bank at the hard-money rate you are charging to your borrower, you gain the benefit of additional PUAs in a participating whole life policy or additional capital added to the cash accumulation value in an IUL policy. Remember that, even during the life of the loan, the amount you've loaned out continues to generate income from paid dividends or interest, or index gains, depending on the type of policy you use to fund your Private Vault. What's more, you will be generating additional reserves in the policy by paying back the loan at a higher-than-required interest rate.

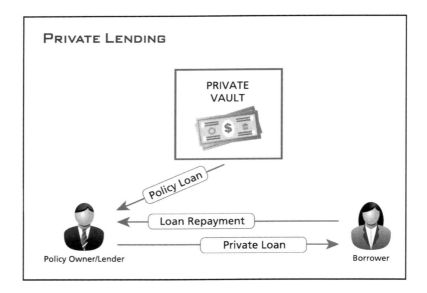

Buying Rental Properties

Now let's look at another kind of real estate investment play: purchasing rental properties. Unlike with rehab investing, banks will typically provide mortgage financing for the purchase of rental properties. But using your private bank is the superior alternative.

Let's look at a hypothetical comparison of financing a rental property purchase through a bank and through your Private Vault.

Todd and Joe are two real estate investors who are embarking on very similar projects, but with different approaches to financing. Each plans to purchase a rental property. For ease of comparison, let's say that the two properties have an identical purchase price of $100,000.

Todd borrows $100,000 from his bank, in the form of a 10-year mortgage at 5% interest. Over the life of the loan, Todd will repay principal and interest to the bank of $132,479. His total interest payments will be $32,479. Once the loan is repaid, Todd will own an asset worth $100,000, and he will have paid $32,479 to finance it. In other words, he will have increased his net worth by $67,521.

Joe, on the other hand, will finance his purchase through his Private Vault. Just like Todd, he will borrow $100,000, structuring his loan for 10 years at 5% interest. Like Todd, Joe will make total payments of $132,479, which includes total interest payments of $32,479. And just like his fellow investor, he will own an asset worth $100,000 and generate passive income for his investment portfolio.

Although their situations are similar, there's a fundamental difference in the total value of Todd and Joe's net worth at the end of the loan contract. Unlike Todd, Joe won't send his hard-earned money to a bank, never to be seen again. He will repay principal and interest to his vault. In the meantime, the cash in his vault will continue to earn a return of 6% or higher. Also remember that Joe will never actually remove cash from his account—he'll simply take a loan using that cash as collateral. As a result, all of his principal will continue to accrue interest.

At the end of 10 years, the cash value within Joe's vault will have grown to $133,225. Not only will he have an asset in the form of a $100,000 rental property, but he will have an even greater cash value within his Private Vault than he started with. By buying that rental property and financing it through his Private Vault, Joe will have increased his net worth by $233,225.

BUYING A RENTAL PROPERTY

—TODD USES A BANK

- Borrow $100k
  - 10-year term at 5%
  - Total payments of **$132,479**

- Value of Rental $100k
  - **No increase in value in the capital he used to finance the transaction**

—JOE USES HIS PRIVATE VAULT

- Borrow $100k
  - 10-year term at 5%
  - Total payments of **$132,479**

- Value of Rental $100k
  - Joe pays his insurance company the interest

- Vault continued to grow at 6%
  - **Vault Increased to: $133,225**

13

Financing
Business Purchases

I f you're a business owner, you've invested a ton into the
enterprise—a lot of blood, sweat, and tears, and probably
a lot of money as well. As an entrepreneur, reinvesting profits
back into your business is usually the name of the game. In
fact, most business owners neglect their own retirement savings in order to focus on growing their business successfully.

In the end, they figure, the *business* is the retirement plan.
It's the nest egg. The more that your business is worth, the
more you'll be able to sell it for, and the more comfortable
you will be in retirement.

Well, your Private Vault can really help to build that nest
egg. Not only can it grow your wealth directly, but it can stop
the flow of wealth from your business to outside financiers.
That will enable your permanent life policy and your business
to prosper in ways that neither could individually.

Let's illustrate how this works by using the example of a
successful plumbing business owned by Ted Johnson. Ted's
business, Jiffy Plumbing, Inc., has a fleet of vans that it uses to

cover an entire county. Naturally, over the years these vehicles wear out and need to be replaced.

Typically, a business like Jiffy Plumbing would use traditional lending sources to finance the purchase of new vans—a bank or its close relative, an auto financing company. Let's say that it's time for Jiffy Plumbing to replace an aging member of its van fleet. Ted goes to his bank and, as he's done several times in the past, applies for an auto loan. The business, not Ted, will technically be the borrower—but as we'll see, Ted will ultimately feel the negative impact of using bank financing to buy this piece of equipment.

The bank, of course, is delighted to extend credit. Jiffy Plumbing is a successful business with a solid credit history. Loaning the company $30,000 over five years at 6% interest will net the bank a tidy profit of $4,799. Ted's business will be able to put a new van into service right away.

But notice the effect of depreciation. After five years of use, the van has depreciated in value from $30,000 to $15,000. On top of that, Jiffy Plumbing will have paid $4,799 of interest by the end of the loan term. The total loss is ugly:

- $15,000 through depreciation of the van

- $4,799 lost through interest payments

- Total loss: $19,799

Consider the amount of wealth Jiffy Plumbing will lose over the years as it replaces van after van. Again, the bank is happy to take receipt of a big chunk of that wealth, but what does the business have to show for it? A steady outflow of wealth and a parking lot full of depreciating assets. Since the business is Ted's nest egg, that's the last thing he wants.

It's enough to make Ted want to just pay cash! But paying cash is a losing proposition too. First of all, spending a business's cash in a depreciating asset is not the best investment you can make. It's true that the van serves a purpose and is necessary for Jiffy Plumbing to operate as a business. But remember, it's still an asset that loses value over time.

Furthermore, when a business deploys its cash to make purchases, it encounters an opportunity cost. Cash can only be used once, for a single purpose—and once it's spent it cannot continue growing and working for us.

What if Ted deployed $30,000 of his company's cash to purchase a van rather than investing it with a rate of return of, say, 5%? With a 5% rate of return, the business would have earned $8,288.45 in interest over five years. Over 10 years, the return would be $18,866.82. Earning these returns is not possible if you've spent your cash. The van dealer might invest Ted's cash and put it to work—but Ted won't be able to! All he will have is a depreciating asset.

We will assume for the purposes of this illustration that by paying cash for the van, Ted's company has sacrificed the possibility of earning 5% interest on that cash. Looking ahead five years after paying cash on the barrel for that van, we can survey the damage:

- $15,000 through depreciation of the van

- $8,288 in opportunity cost (losing the opportunity to invest the $30,000 cash)

- Total loss: $23,288

More than $23,000 is lost in just five years. And remember, it's not just some business that lost this wealth—it's Ted.

Ted's business is his retirement plan! The prosperity of the business is directly related to the amount of money that Ted will ultimately be able to sell it for. In a sense, that $23,000 needlessly sacrificed on the van purchase is coming right out of Ted's future.

But there's another possibility. What if Ted's business could obtain the van it needs without taking a bank loan, and without spending cash? That's where Ted's Private Vault comes in.

Lending to Your Business

If instead of using bank financing, what if Jiffy Plumbing were to buy vehicles using financing from the private bank of its owner, Ted? Here's how this scenario would work:

Ted, not his business, owns a permanent life insurance policy that serves as Ted's private bank. The next time a plumbing van needs to be replaced, Ted bypasses his bank, and makes the loan from his Private Vault. He will be the banker to his own company.

Ted puts on his banker hat to take care of a few pieces of business. First, he makes sure that his company has sufficient cash flow to repay the $30,000 auto loan he's about to make.

He then creates an amortization schedule, templates are easily found online, by plugging in principal, an interest rate, and number of payments. The schedule will calculate the total payment that his business will ultimately make to him. Ted also has the business sign a promissory note (again, sample promissory notes are easily available on the Internet). A simple promissory note adds a layer of legal protection and may also result in tax benefits for lender and borrower.

One of Ted's responsibilities as lender will be to set an interest rate. This is where it gets fun. As the "banker," Ted can charge a bit more than the going rate charged by banks. All the interest above and beyond the rate that Ted's insurance company charges for his policy loan will be "profit." Furthermore, Ted's policy is set up so that this "profit" will be plowed into buying new paid-up additions for a whole life policy or additional cash contributions for an IUL policy. The PUAs increase the size of his death benefit, which results in higher dividend payments from the insurance company into his account. In an IUL policy, the additional cash value increases the amount that can be either allocated to investing in the index account or receiving a guaranteed interest rate in the cash account.

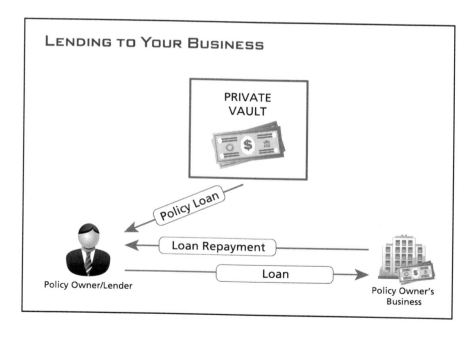

Remember, even while the $30,000 loan is outstanding from Ted's insurance policy, he continues to earn a rate of return—let's say it's 5%—on the entire cash value within his account. That's because Ted's cash does not at any point leave his account: It merely serves as collateral for the policy loan that is extended by his insurance company. In fact, over five years, the $30,000 that remains in Ted's account will gather interest of $8,288.

Fast forward five years and take stock of how this has worked out for Jiffy Plumbing and its owner. Remember, financing through the bank resulted in an effective loss of $19,799, and paying cash resulted in an effective loss of $23,288. But financing through Ted's Private Vault created a completely different result:

- Principal repaid to Ted's Private Vault: $30,000

- Excess repayment of interest in Ted's policy: $1,698

- Return on the $30,000 in Ted's account @5%: $8,288

- Value of van after five years: $15,000

- Total assets gained: **$54,986**

The Leasing Advantage

Many businesses use leasing companies as a means to protect their assets from lawsuits and creditors. This approach can be used by small and mid-sized businesses as well—and it can work hand-in-glove with the Private Vault financing that we've been discussing. Be sure to consult your attorney or accountant before implementing any of what I'm about to describe.

Let's assume your business wants to shield its assets from any potential lawsuits or creditor claims in the future. You set up a limited liability company to serve as a leasing company. The leasing company buys everything—from equipment to automobiles to furniture—and leases them to the original business.

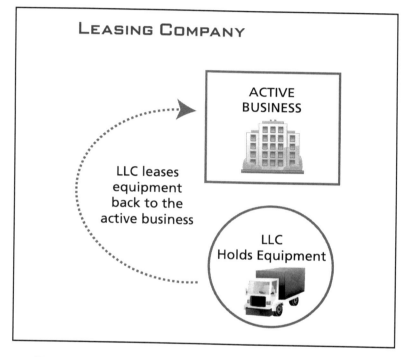

LEASING COMPANY

ACTIVE BUSINESS

LLC leases equipment back to the active business

LLC Holds Equipment

Because your business leases its equipment from the leasing company, it has little or no physical assets that might be seized by creditors or courts. In fact, using leasing arrangements often discourages creditors from suing in the first place, since there would be little to gain. And to the extent that your business assets are not vulnerable to seizure, your nest egg, in the form of your business, is insulated.

Again, it's important to consult the proper professionals before pursuing a leasing company strategy. Many large companies see a benefit in using this strategy, so it is worth exploring.

Now, how does the leasing company buy the equipment that it will lease to your company? It finances it through your Private Vault, of course. Once again, you'll put on your banker's hat, making sure there's adequate cash flow to sustain repayment of the loan. You'll set up an amortization schedule, and you'll obtain a signed promissory note.

Since you'll be setting the terms of the loan, you'll charge an interest-rate premium above and beyond the rate on your policy loan, in order to more quickly grow the value of your Private Vault.

Using Your Business to Fund Your Vault

Thus far we have focused only on using your personal funds to contribute to your Private Vault. However, properly structured use of your Private Vault can create phenomenal deductions for your business while setting aside wealth to finance purchases and provide for your retirement.

Ted, like many business owners, wanted to plan for his retirement and to provide a retirement benefit for his loyal employees. To achieve this, his company adopted a 401(k) plan that allowed he and his employees to contribute. Ted's business also made a 3% matching contribution, which created an additional tax deduction for his business.

Ted wanted to be able to stash more funds away for his retirement, but to do so would obligate his business to also make similar contributions for his employees. Unfortunately, this would have created too great of a financial strain on the company. Thankfully, Ted had spoken with his insurance specialist regarding this very issue. In fact, that conversation was

Ted's first exposure to the use of permanent insurance to meet his needs.

John, Ted's insurance specialist, detailed a plan using permanent insurance owned by Ted but funded by Ted's company, Jiffy Plumbing, Inc. The premium payments that Jiffy Plumbing made on Ted's behalf would be treated as a tax-deductible contribution for the business.

Since the insurance policy was not a qualified retirement plan, Ted's business would not have to make contributions to policies set up for his employees. The policy would be structured to solely benefit the company's executive, Ted, and create additional tax deductions for the company. However, there was a catch: although the premium payments were deductible to the business, the money was treated as taxable income to Ted.

Ted had two choices. He could borrow annually from his Private Vault to cover the tax liability on contributions made by his company. Or, the company could set aside an amount to cover Ted's tax liability. Since one of Ted's planning objectives was to use the funds in his Private Vault as a lending source for his fleet of plumbing vans, he did not want to be in the position of needing to take additional loans from his vault to cover his tax liability. Thus, Ted decided to have his premium payments structured as an executive bonus plan through his company.

In order for his vault to have sufficient cash to consistently provide a funding source for the company's van purchases, Ted elected to pay a $30,000 annual premium. However, the premium payments would come directly from Jiffy Plumbing, and not from Ted personally. Since Ted is required to treat these premium payments as taxable income, it was essential that additional funds be set aside to cover Ted's tax liability. Jiffy Plumbing decided to pay Ted an annual executive bonus of $42,857. The payment was a deductible expense to the company.

Ted happens to be in the 30% income tax bracket. Therefore, in order to cover his tax liability, $12,857 of the bonus was set aside to pay Ted's taxes on the funds. The remaining $30,000 constituted his annual premium for his Private Vault. Since Ted created his Private Vault when he was 40, by the time he retires at age 66, he will receive $137,000 tax-free as an annual policy loan from his Private Vault until he reaches age 100.

This strategy has achieved Ted's goals of:

- Providing a private funding source for the purchase of his company vans

- Setting aside more funds for his own retirement without having to cover his employees, and

- Providing a death benefit to his family.

14

Conclusion

Financial peace of mind is elusive in today's world. As the old pension system crumbles, most of us find ourselves in charge of paying for our own retirement.

It's a daunting task. Faced with economic and market volatility, along with taxes and inflation, many Americans are investing their savings and hoping for the best. And unfortunately, the financial industry to which we turn for tools and guidance offers us a narrow and often self-serving range of solutions, from 529 college savings plans to mortgages to 401(k)s.

My purpose in writing this book has been to let you know that you can do better. You don't have to live with uncertainty. You don't have to bet your future on risky investments and spend your valuable resources enriching bankers and Wall Street firms.

You have within your reach an alternative solution that replaces question marks with predictability, one that provides a proven way to keep your wealth, build your wealth, and achieve financial independence. By creating your own Private

Vault, you can take back control over your future—and, in the process, you can ensure a legacy for those you love.

So what now? Remember that each Private Vault is built around an insurance solution that is custom-designed according to your situation and your goals. Because there is no off-the-shelf solution, it's important to deal with an experienced insurance expert whom you trust. And keep in mind that the best aren't simply interested in simply selling insurance solutions—they're committed to helping you reach your goals and achieve true financial independence.

At Anderson Financial Services, LLC, we work with our clients to create an individualized solution to build a solid financial foundation—both now and in the future. We are happy to provide a complimentary consultation to explore your objectives and planning options. To arrange yours, simply contact us using the information below.

ANDERSON
Financial Services, LLC

∾

732 Broadway, Suite 201
Tacoma, WA 98402
888.473.6931 (Main)
253.238.0003 (Fax)
info@afsplan.com

Appendix A

26 USC Section 7702

26 USC Section 7702 – Life insurance contract defined.

(a) General rule

For purposes of this title, the term "life insurance contract" means any contract which is a life insurance contract under the applicable law, but only if such contract—

> **(1) meets the cash value accumulation test of subsection (b), or**
>
> **(2)**
>> (A) meets the guideline premium requirements of subsection (c), and
>>
>> (B) falls within the cash value corridor of subsection (d).

(b) Cash value accumulation test for subsection (a)(1)

> **(1) In general**
> A contract meets the cash value accumulation test of this subsection if, by the terms of the contract, the cash surrender value of such contract may not at any time exceed the net single premium which would have to be paid at such time to fund future benefits under the contract.

> **(2) Rules for applying paragraph (1)**
> Determinations under paragraph (1) shall be made—

(A) on the basis of interest at the greater of an annual effective rate of 4 percent or the rate or rates guaranteed on issuance of the contract,

(B) on the basis of the rules of subparagraph (B)(i) (and, in the case of qualified additional benefits, subparagraph (B)(ii)) of subsection (c)(3), and

(C) by taking into account under subparagraphs (A) and (D) of subsection (e)(1) only current and future death benefits and qualified additional benefits.

(c) Guideline premium requirements

For purposes of this section—

(1) In general
A contract meets the guideline premium requirements of this subsection if the sum of the premiums paid under such contract does not at any time exceed the guideline premium limitation as of such time.

(2) Guideline premium limitation
The term "guideline premium limitation" means, as of any date, the greater of—

(A) the guideline single premium, or

(B) the sum of the guideline level premiums to such date.

(3) Guideline single premium

(A) In general
The term "guideline single premium" means the premium at issue with respect to future benefits under the contract.

(B) Basis on which determination is made
The determination under subparagraph (A) shall be based on—

(i) reasonable mortality charges which meet the

requirements (if any) prescribed in regulations and which (except as provided in regulations) do not exceed the mortality charges specified in the prevailing commissioners' standard tables (as defined in section 807(d)(5)) as of the time the contract is issued,

(ii) any reasonable charges (other than mortality charges) which (on the basis of the company's experience, if any, with respect to similar contracts) are reasonably expected to be actually paid, and

(iii) interest at the greater of an annual effective rate of 6 percent or the rate or rates guaranteed on issuance of the contract.

(C) When determination made

Except as provided in subsection (f)(7), the determination under subparagraph (A) shall be made as of the time the contract is issued.

(D) Special rules for subparagraph (B)(ii)

(i) Charges not specified in the contract

If any charge is not specified in the contract, the amount taken into account under subparagraph (B)(ii) for such charge shall be zero.

(ii) New companies, etc.

If any company does not have adequate experience for purposes of the determination under subparagraph (B)(ii), to the extent provided in regulations, such determination shall be made on the basis of the industry-wide experience.

(4) Guideline level premium

The term "guideline level premium" means the level annual amount, payable over a period not ending before the insured attains age 95, computed on the same basis as the guideline single premium, except that paragraph (3)(B)(iii) shall be applied by substituting "4 percent" for "6 percent".

(d) Cash value corridor for purposes of subsection (a)(2)(B)

For purposes of this section—

(1) In general

A contract falls within the cash value corridor of this subsection if the death benefit under the contract at any time is not less than the applicable percentage of the cash surrender value.

(2) Applicable percentage

In the case of an insured with an attained age as of the beginning of the contract year of:		The applicable percentage shall decrease by a ratable portion for each fully year:	
More than:	But not more than	From:	To:
0 40		250 250	
40 45		250 215	
45 50		215 185	
50 55		185 150	
55 60		150 130	
60 65		130 120	
65 70		120 115	
70 75		115 105	
75 90		105 105	
90 95		105 .... 100.	

(e) Computational rules

(1) In general

For purposes of this section (other than subsection (d))—

(A) the death benefit (and any qualified additional benefit) shall be deemed not to increase,

(B) the maturity date, including the date on which any benefit described in subparagraph (C) is payable, shall be deemed to be no earlier than the day on which the insured attains age 95, and no later than the day on which the insured attains age 100,

(C) the death benefits shall be deemed to be provided until the maturity date determined by taking into account subparagraph (B), and

(D) the amount of any endowment benefit (or sum of endowment benefits, including any cash surrender value on the maturity date determined by taking into account subparagraph (B)) shall be deemed not to exceed the least amount payable as a death benefit at any time under the contract.

(2) Limited increases in death benefit permitted
Notwithstanding paragraph (1)(A)—

(A) for purposes of computing the guideline level premium, an increase in the death benefit which is provided in the contract may be taken into account but only to the extent necessary to prevent a decrease in the excess of the death benefit over the cash surrender value of the contract,

(B) for purposes of the cash value accumulation test, the increase described in subparagraph (A) may be taken into account if the contract will meet such test at all times assuming that the net level reserve (determined as if level annual premiums were paid for the contract over a period not ending before the insured attains age 95) is substituted for the net single premium, and

(C) for purposes of the cash value accumulation test, the death benefit increases may be taken into account if the contract—

(i) has an initial death benefit of $5,000 or less and a maximum death benefit of $25,000 or less,

(ii) provides for a fixed predetermined annual increase not to exceed 10 percent of the initial death benefit or 8 percent of the death benefit at the end of the preceding year, and

(iii) was purchased to cover payment of burial expenses or in connection with prearranged funeral expenses.

For purposes of subparagraph (C), the initial death benefit of a contract shall be determined by treating all contracts issued to the same contract owner as 1 contract.

(f) Other definitions and special rules

For purposes of this section—

(1) Premiums paid

(A) In general
The term "premiums paid" means the premiums paid under the contract less amounts (other than amounts includible in gross income) to which section 72 (e) applies and less any excess premiums with respect to which there is a distribution described in subparagraph (B) or (E) of paragraph (7) and any other amounts received with respect to the contract which are specified in regulations.

(B) Treatment of certain premiums returned to policy-holder
If, in order to comply with the requirements of subsection (a)(2)(A), any portion of any premium paid during any contract year is returned by the insurance company (with interest) within 60 days after the end of a contract year, the amount so returned (excluding interest) shall be deemed to reduce the sum of the premiums paid under the contract during such year.

(C) Interest returned includible in gross income
Notwithstanding the provisions of section 72 (e), the amount of any interest returned as provided in subparagraph (B) shall be includible in the gross income of the recipient.

(2) Cash values

(A) Cash surrender value

The cash surrender value of any contract shall be its cash value determined without regard to any surrender charge, policy loan, or reasonable termination dividends.

(B) Net surrender value

The net surrender value of any contract shall be determined with regard to surrender charges but without regard to any policy loan.

(3) Death benefit

The term "death benefit" means the amount payable by reason of the death of the insured (determined without regard to any qualified additional benefits).

(4) Future benefits

The term "future benefits" means death benefits and endowment benefits.

(5) Qualified additional benefits

(A) In general

The term "qualified additional benefits" means any—

(i) guaranteed insurability,

(ii) accidental death or disability benefit,

(iii) family term coverage,

(iv) disability waiver benefit, or

(v) other benefit prescribed under regulations.

(B) Treatment of qualified additional benefits

For purposes of this section, qualified additional benefits shall not be treated as future benefits under the contract, but the charges for such benefits shall be treated as future benefits.

(C) Treatment of other additional benefits

In the case of any additional benefit which is not a qualified additional benefit—

> (i) such benefit shall not be treated as a future benefit, and

> (ii) any charge for such benefit which is not prefunded shall not be treated as a premium.

(6) Premium payments not disqualifying contract

The payment of a premium which would result in the sum of the premiums paid exceeding the guideline premium limitation shall be disregarded for purposes of subsection (a)(2) if the amount of such premium does not exceed the amount necessary to prevent the termination of the contract on or before the end of the contract year (but only if the contract will have no cash surrender value at the end of such extension period).

(7) Adjustments

(A) In general

If there is a change in the benefits under (or in other terms of) the contract which was not reflected in any previous determination or adjustment made under this section, there shall be proper adjustments in future determinations made under this section.

(B) Rule for certain changes during first 15 years

If—

> (i) a change described in subparagraph (A) reduces benefits under the contract,

> (ii) the change occurs during the 15-year period beginning on the issue date of the contract, and

> (iii) a cash distribution is made to the policyholder as a result of such change,

> section 72 (other than subsection (e)(5) thereof) shall

apply to such cash distribution to the extent it does not exceed the recapture ceiling determined under subparagraph (C) or (D) (whichever applies).

(C) Recapture ceiling where change occurs during first 5 years

If the change referred to in subparagraph (B)(ii) occurs during the 5-year period beginning on the issue date of the contract, the recapture ceiling is—

> (i) in the case of a contract to which subsection (a)(1) applies, the excess of—
>
>> (I) the cash surrender value of the contract, immediately before the reduction, over
>> (II) the net single premium (determined under subsection (b)), immediately after the reduction, or
>
> (ii) in the case of a contract to which subsection (a)(2) applies, the greater of—
>
>> (I) the excess of the aggregate premiums paid under the contract, immediately before the reduction, over the guideline premium limitation for the contract (determined under subsection (c)(2), taking into account the adjustment described in subparagraph (A)), or
>> (II) the excess of the cash surrender value of the contract, immediately before the reduction, over the cash value corridor of subsection (d) (determined immediately after the reduction).

(D) Recapture ceiling where change occurs after 5th year and before 16th year

If the change referred to in subparagraph (B) occurs after the 5-year period referred to under subparagraph (C), the recapture ceiling is the excess of the cash surrender value of the contract, immediately before the reduction, over the cash value corridor of subsection (d) (determined immediately after the reduction and whether or not subsection (d) applies to the contract).

(E) Treatment of certain distributions made in anticipation of benefit reductions

Under regulations prescribed by the Secretary, subparagraph (B) shall apply also to any distribution made in anticipation of a reduction in benefits under the contract. For purposes of the preceding sentence, appropriate adjustments shall be made in the provisions of subparagraphs (C) and (D); and any distribution which reduces the cash surrender value of a contract and which is made within 2 years before a reduction in benefits under the contract shall be treated as made in anticipation of such reduction.

(8) Correction of errors

If the taxpayer establishes to the satisfaction of the Secretary that—

(A) the requirements described in subsection (a) for any contract year were not satisfied due to reasonable error, and

(B) reasonable steps are being taken to remedy the error,

the Secretary may waive the failure to satisfy such requirements.

(9) Special rule for variable life insurance contracts

In the case of any contract which is a variable contract (as defined in section 817), the determination of whether such contract meets the requirements of subsection (a) shall be made whenever the death benefits under such contract change but not less frequently than once during each 12-month period.

(g) Treatment of contracts which do not meet subsection (a) test

(1) Income inclusion

(A) In general

If at any time any contract which is a life insurance contract under the applicable law does not meet the definition of life insurance contract under subsection (a), the income on the contract for any taxable year of the policyholder shall be treated as ordinary income received or accrued by the policyholder during such year.

(B) Income on the contract

For purposes of this paragraph, the term "income on the contract" means, with respect to any taxable year of the policyholder, the excess of—

> (i) the sum of—
>
>> (I) the increase in the net surrender value of the contract during the taxable year, and
>> (II) the cost of life insurance protection provided under the contract during the taxable year, over
>
> (ii) the premiums paid (as defined in subsection (f) (1)) under the contract during the taxable year.

(C) Contracts which cease to meet definition

If, during any taxable year of the policyholder, a contract which is a life insurance contract under the applicable law ceases to meet the definition of life insurance contract under subsection (a), the income on the contract for all prior taxable years shall be treated as received or accrued during the taxable year in which such cessation occurs.

(D) Cost of life insurance protection

For purposes of this paragraph, the cost of life insurance protection provided under the contract shall be the lesser of—

> (i) the cost of individual insurance on the life of the insured as determined on the basis of uniform premiums (computed on the basis of 5-year age brackets) prescribed by the Secretary by regulations, or
>
> (ii) the mortality charge (if any) stated in the contract.

(2) Treatment of amount paid on death of insured

If any contract which is a life insurance contract under the applicable law does not meet the definition of life insurance contract under subsection (a), the excess of the amount paid by the reason of the death of the insured over the net surrender value of the contract shall be deemed to be paid under a life insurance contract for purposes of section <u>101</u> and subtitle B.

(3) Contract continues to be treated as insurance contract

If any contract which is a life insurance contract under the applicable law does not meet the definition of life insurance contract under subsection (a), such contract shall, notwithstanding such failure, be treated as an insurance contract for purposes of this title.

(h) Endowment contracts receive same treatment

(1) In general

References in subsections (a) and (g) to a life insurance contract shall be treated as including references to a contract which is an endowment contract under the applicable law.

(2) Definition of endowment contract

For purposes of this title (other than paragraph (1)), the term "endowment contract" means a contract which is an endowment contract under the applicable law and which meets the requirements of subsection (a).

(i) Transitional rule for certain 20-pay contracts

(1) In general

In the case of a qualified 20-pay contract, this section shall be applied by substituting "3 percent" for "4 percent" in subsection (b)(2).

(2) Qualified 20-pay contract

For purposes of paragraph (1), the term "qualified 20-pay contract" means any contract which—

(A) requires at least 20 nondecreasing annual premium payments, and

(B) is issued pursuant to an existing plan of insurance.

(3) Existing plan of insurance

For purposes of this subsection, the term "existing plan of insurance" means, with respect to any contract, any plan of insurance which was filed by the company issuing such contract in 1 or more States before September 28, 1983, and is on file in the appropriate State for such contract.

(j) Certain church self-funded death benefit plans treated as life insurance

(1) In general

In determining whether any plan or arrangement described in paragraph (2) is a life insurance contract, the requirement of subsection (a) that the contract be a life insurance contract under applicable law shall not apply.

(2) Description

For purposes of this subsection, a plan or arrangement is described in this paragraph if—

(A) such plan or arrangement provides for the payment of benefits by reason of the death of the individuals covered under such plan or arrangement, and

(B) such plan or arrangement is provided by a church for the benefit of its employees and their beneficiaries, directly or through an organization described in section 414 (e)(3) (A) or an organization described in section 414 (e)(3)(B) (ii).

(3) Definitions

For purposes of this subsection—

(A) Church

The term "church" means a church or a convention or association of churches.

(B) Employee
The term "employee" includes an employee described in section 414 (e)(3)(B).

(k) Regulations

The Secretary shall prescribe such regulations as may be necessary or appropriate to carry out the purposes of this section.

Appendix B

Overview of Creditor Protection Laws for Life Insurance and Annuities

Alabama

Life Insurance:

Proceeds and avails of life insurance are exempt.

Alabama Code – Section 6-10-8 – Rights of beneficiaries and assignees under fife insurance policies.

If a policy of insurance, whether heretofore or hereafter issued, is effected by any person on his or her own life or on another life in favor of a person other than himself or herself or, except in cases of transfer with intent to defraud creditors, if a policy of life insurance is assigned or in any way made payable to any such person, the lawful beneficiary or assignee thereof, other than the insured or the person so effecting such insurance, or his or her executors or administrators, shall be entitled to its proceeds and avails against the creditors and representatives of the insured and of the person effecting the same, whether or not the right to change the beneficiary is reserved or permitted and whether or not the policy is made payable to the person whose life is insured if the beneficiary or assignee shall predecease such person; provided, that subject to the statute of limitations, the amount of any premiums for said insurance paid with intent to defraud creditors, with interest thereon, shall inure to their benefit from the proceeds of the policy; but the company issuing the policy shall be discharged of all liability thereon by payment of its proceeds in accordance with its terms unless, before such payment, the company shall have written notice, by or in behalf of a creditor, of a claim to recover for transfer made or premiums paid with intent to defraud creditors, with specifications of the amount claimed. A husband or a wife, in his or her own name or in the name of a trustee, may insure the life of his or her spouse for the benefit of himself or herself, or for the benefit of himself or herself and any child or children of the marriage; or a husband or a wife may insure his or her own life for the benefit of his or her spouse, or for the benefit of his or her spouse and children, or for the benefit of their children, either in the names of such children or in the name of a trustee; and such insurance and the proceeds and avails thereof, whether or not the right to change the beneficiary is reserved or permitted, is exempt from liability for the debts or engagements of the insured, or for the torts of the insured, or for any penalty or damages recoverable of the insured.

Annuity Contract:

Benefits, rights, privileges and options under an annuity contract are exempt up to $250 per month.

Alabama Code – Section 27-14-32 – Exemption from debt of proceeds – annuity contracts.

(a) The benefits, rights, privileges, and options which under any annuity contract, heretofore or hereafter issued, are due or prospectively due the annuitant shall not be subject to execution, nor shall the annuitant be compelled to exercise any such rights, powers, or options, nor shall creditors be allowed to interfere with or terminate the contract, except:

(1) As to amounts paid for or as premium on any such annuity with intent to defraud creditors, with interest thereon, and of which the creditor has given the insurer written notice at its home office prior to the making of the payments to the annuitant out of which the creditor seeks to recover. Any such notice shall specify the amount claimed, or such facts as will enable the insurer to ascertain such amount, and shall set forth such facts as will enable the insurer to

ascertain the insurance or annuity contract, the person insured or annuitant and the payments sought to be avoided on the ground of fraud;

(2) The total exemption of benefits presently due and payable to any annuitant periodically or at stated times under all annuity contracts under which he is an annuitant shall not at any time exceed $250.00 per month for the length of time represented by such installments, and such periodic payments in excess of $250.00 per month shall be subject to garnishment;

(3) If the total benefits presently due and payable to any annuitant under all annuity contracts under which he is an annuitant shall at any time exceed payment at the rate of $250.00 per month, then the court may order such annuitant to pay to a judgment creditor or apply on the judgment, in installments, such portion of such excess benefits as to the court may appear just and proper, after due regard for the reasonable requirements of the judgment debtor and his family, if dependent upon him, as well as any payments required to be made by the annuitant to other creditors under prior court orders.

(b) If the contract so provides, the benefits, rights, privileges, or options accruing under such contract to a beneficiary or assignee shall not be transferable nor subject to commutation, and if the benefits are payable periodically or at stated times, the same exemptions and exceptions contained in this section for the annuitant shall apply with respect to such beneficiary or assignee.

Alaska

Life Insurance and Annuity Contract:

Unmatured life insurance and annuity contracts owned by the debtor are exempt. If the debtor has accrued more than $10,000 a creditor may obtain a court order requiring the payment of the accrued amount over $10,000.

Alaska Statutes – Section 09.38.025 – Exemption of unmatured life insurance and annuity contracts.

(a) Except as provided in this section or AS 09.38.017, an individual is entitled to exemption of unmatured life insurance and annuity contracts owned by the individual. If the contracts have accrued dividends and loan values available to the individual aggregating more than $10,000, a creditor may obtain a court order requiring the individual debtor to pay the creditor, and authorizing the creditor on the debtor's behalf to obtain payment of, the amount of the accrued dividends and loan values in excess of $10,000 or the amount of the creditor's claim, whichever is less.

(b) A judgment creditor or other claimant of an insurer may not levy upon any of the assets or securities held in this state as a deposit for the protection of the insurer's policyholders or policyholders and creditors. Deposits under AS 21.09.270 may be levied upon if provided in the order of the director of insurance, Department of Commerce, Community, and Economic Development, under which the deposit is made.

Arizona

Life Insurance:

Proceeds and avails of life insurance are exempt.

Arizona Revised Statutes – Section 20-1131 – Exemption of life insurance proceeds and cash values from creditors.

A. If a policy of life insurance is effected by any person on the person's own life or on another life in favor of another person having an insurable interest in the policy, or made payable by assignment, change of beneficiary or other means to a third person, the lawful beneficiary or such third person, other than the person effecting the insurance or the person's legal representatives, is entitled to its proceeds against the creditors and representatives of the person effecting the insurance.

B. Subject to the statute of limitations, the amount of any premiums for insurance paid in fraud of creditors, with interest, shall inure to their benefit from the proceeds of the policy, but the insurer issuing the policy shall be discharged of all liability on the policy by payment of the proceeds in accordance with its terms, unless before payment the insurer received written notice by or in behalf of some creditor, with specification of the amount claimed, claiming to recover for certain premiums paid in fraud of creditors.

C. For the purposes of subsection A, a policy shall also be deemed to be payable to a person other than the insured if and to the extent that a facility-of-payment clause or similar clause in the policy permits the insurer to discharge its obligation after the death of the individual insured by paying the death benefits to a person as permitted by the clause.

D. If, for a continuous, unexpired period of two years, a policy of life insurance has named as beneficiary the insured's surviving spouse, child, parent, brother, sister or any other dependent family member, then, in event of bankruptcy or in any proceeding before any court in this state, the cash surrender value of the insurance, in the proportion that the policy names any such beneficiary, shall be exempt from claims and demands of all creditors, other than a creditor to whom the policy has been pledged or assigned, and except that, subject to the statute of limitations, the amount of any premiums which are recoverable or avoidable by a creditor pursuant to title 44, chapter 8, article 1, with interest, shall inure to their benefit from the cash surrender value. For the purposes of this subsection, "dependent" means a family member who is dependent on the insured for not less than half support.

Insurance: Arizona Revised Statutes – Section 20-1126 (A) (1) & (A)(6) – Money benefits or proceeds; exception

A. The following property of a debtor is exempt from execution, attachment or sale on any process issued from any court:

> 1. All money received by or payable to a surviving spouse or child on the life of a deceased spouse, parent or legal guardian, not exceeding twenty thousand dollars.

6. The cash surrender value of life insurance policies where for a continuous unexpired period of two years the policies have been owned by a debtor. The policy shall have named as beneficiary the debtor's surviving spouse, child, parent, brother or sister. The policy may have named as beneficiary any other family member who is a dependent, in the proportion that the policy names any such beneficiary, except that, subject to the statute of limitations, the amount of any premium that is recoverable or avoidable by a creditor pursuant to title 44, chapter 8, article 1, with interest thereon, is not exempt. The exemption provided by this paragraph does not apply to a claim for the payment of a debt of the insured or beneficiary that is secured by a pledge or assignment of the cash value of the insurance policy or the proceeds of the policy. For the purposes of this paragraph, "dependent" means a family member who is dependent on the insured debtor for not less than half support.

Annuity Contract:

Annuity contracts are exempt from creditor claims.

Arizona Revised Statutes – Section 20-1126 (A)(7) – Money benefits or proceeds; exception

A. The following property of a debtor is exempt from execution, attachment or sale on any process issued from any court:

7. An annuity contract where for a continuous unexpired period of two years that contract has been owned by a debtor and has named as beneficiary the debtor, the debtor's surviving spouse, child, parent, brother or sister, or any other dependent family member, except that, subject to the statute of limitations, the amount of any premium, payment or deposit with respect to that contract is recoverable or avoidable by a creditor pursuant to title 44, chapter 8, article 1 is not exempt. The exemption provided by this paragraph does not apply to a claim for a payment of a debt of the annuitant or beneficiary that is secured by a pledge or assignment of the contract or its proceeds. For the purposes of this paragraph, "dependent"

means a family member who is dependent on the debtor for not less than half support.

Arkansas

Life Insurance:

Life insurance proceeds are exempt from creditor claims.

2012 Arkansas Code – Section 23-79-131 – Exemption of proceeds – Life Insurance

(a) (1) If a policy of insurance is effected by any person on his or her own life or on another life in favor of a person other than himself or herself or, except in cases of transfer with intent to defraud creditors, if a policy of life insurance is assigned or in any way made payable to the person, the lawful beneficiary or assignee of the policy, other than the insured or the person effecting the insurance or executors or administrators of the insured or the person effecting the insurance, shall be entitled to its proceeds and avails against the creditors and representatives of the insured and those of the person effecting the policy whether or not the right to change the beneficiary is reserved or permitted and whether or not the policy is made payable to the person whose life is insured, if the beneficiary or assignee shall predecease such a person.

(2) However, subject to the statute of limitations, the amount of any premiums for the insurance paid with intent to defraud creditors, including interest thereon, shall enure to their benefit from the proceeds of the policy, but the insurer issuing the policy shall be discharged of all liability thereof by payment of its proceeds in accordance with its terms unless, before the payment, the insurer shall have written notice at its home office, by or in behalf of a creditor, of a claim to recover for transfer made or premiums paid with intent to defraud creditors, with specifications of the amount so claimed.

(b) For the purposes of subsection (a) of this section, a policy shall also be deemed to be payable to a person other than the insured if, and to the extent that, a facility-of-payment clause or similar clause in the policy permits the insurer to discharge its obligation after the death of the individual insured by paying the death benefits to a person as permitted by the clause.

Annuity Contract:

Benefits, rights, privileges and options under an annuity contract are exempt.

2012 Arkansas Code – Section 23-79-134 – Annuity contracts – Assignability of rights

(a) Benefits, rights, privileges, and options under any annuity or variable annuity contract, which are due or prospectively due the annuitant, shall not be subject to execution, attachment, or garnishment, nor shall the annuitant be compelled to exercise the rights, powers, or options under the contract, nor shall creditors be allowed to interfere with or terminate the contract except:

(1) As to amounts paid for any annuity or variable annuity with intent to defraud creditors, including interest thereon, and of which the creditor has given the insurer written notice at its home office prior to the making of payments to the annuitant out of which the creditor seeks to recover. The notice shall specify the amount claimed, or such facts as will enable the insurer to ascertain the amount, and shall set forth such facts as will enable the insurer to ascertain the insurance or annuity contract, the person insured or annuitant, and the payments sought to be avoided on the ground of fraud; and

(2) If the total benefits presently due and payable to any annuitant under all annuity contracts under which he or she is an annuitant shall at any time exceed the exemptions granted an annuitant by law, a court of appropriate jurisdiction may order the annuitant to pay to a judgment creditor or apply on the judgment, in installments, such portion of the excess benefits as to the court may appear just and proper, after due

regard for the reasonable requirements of the judgment debtor and his or her family, if dependent upon him or her, as well as any payments required to be made by the annuitant to other creditors under prior court orders.

(b) If the contract so provides, the benefits, rights, privileges, or options accruing under the contract to a beneficiary or assignee shall not be transferable nor subject to commutation, and, if the benefits are payable periodically or at stated times, the same exemptions and exceptions contained in this section for the annuitant shall apply with respect to the beneficiary or assignee.

California

Life Insurance & Annuity Contract:

Unmatured life insurance and annuity contracts are exempt up to $9,700 for an individual and $19,400 for a married couple.

Matured life insurance and annuity contracts are exempt to the extent reasonably necessary for the support of the judgment debtor, spouse and dependents.

California Code Of Civil Procedure – Section 704.100

(a) Unmatured life insurance policies (including endowment and annuity policies), but not the loan value of such policies, are exempt without making a claim.

(b) The aggregate loan value of unmatured life insurance policies (including endowment and annuity policies) is subject to the enforcement of a money judgment but is exempt in the amount of nine thousand seven hundred dollars ($9,700). If the judgment debtor is married, each spouse is entitled to a separate exemption under this subdivision, and the exemptions of the spouses may be combined, regardless of whether the policies belong to either or both spouses and regardless of whether the spouse of the judgment debtor is also a judgment debtor under the judgment. The exemption provided by this subdivision shall be first applied to policies other than the policy before the court and then, if the exemption is not exhausted, to the policy before the court.

(c) Benefits from matured life insurance policies (including endowment and annuity policies) are exempt to the extent reasonably necessary for the support of the judgment debtor and the spouse and dependents of the judgment debtor.

Colorado

Life Insurance:

Cash surrender value of up to $100,000 are exempt. There is no exemption for increase in cash value during forty-eight months prior to the writ of attachment or writ of execution.

Colorado Revised Statutes – Section 12.54.102 (1)(l) – Property Exempt

The following property is exempt from levy and sale under writ of attachment or writ of execution:

(I)

(A) The cash surrender value of policies or certificates of life insurance to the extent of one hundred thousand dollars for writs of attachment or writs of execution issued against the insured; except that there is no exemption for increases in cash value from moneys contributed to a policy or certificate of life insurance during the forty-eight months prior to the issuance of the writ of attachment or writ of execution; and

(B) The proceeds of policies or certificates of life insurance paid upon the death of the insured to a designated beneficiary, without limitation as to amount, for writs of attachment or writs of execution issued against the insured.

(II) The provisions of this paragraph (l) shall not be interpreted to provide an exemption for attachment or execution of the proceeds of any policy or certificate of life insurance to pay the debts of a beneficiary of such policy or certificate.

(III) The provisions of this paragraph (l) shall not provide an exemption for attachment or execution of the proceeds of any policy or certificate of life insurance if the beneficiary of such policy or certificate is the estate of the insured.

Annuity Contract: No Specific Statute

Connecticut

Life Insurance and Annuity Contract:

Proceeds of life insurance policies are exempt.

Up to $4,000 is exempt in an unmatured life policy.

Proceeds of life insurance policies and annuity contracts held in trust are exempt.

Connecticut General Statutes – Section 52-352b(s) – Exempt Property

The following property of any natural person shall be exempt:

(s) Any interest of the exemptioner not to exceed in value four thousand dollars in any accrued dividend or interest under, or loan value of, any unmatured life insurance contract owned by the exemptioner under which the insured is the exemptioner or an individual of whom the exemptioner is a dependent;

Life Insurance and Annuity Contract: Connecticut General Statutes – Section 38a-154

Proceeds of insurance policies and annuities may be held in trust. Any domestic life insurance company shall have power to hold the proceeds of any policy issued by it under a trust or other agreement upon such terms and restrictions as to revocation by the policyholder and control by beneficiaries and with such exemptions from the claims of creditors of beneficiaries other than the policyholder as have been agreed to in writing by such company and the policyholder. Such insurance company shall not be required to segregate funds so held but may hold them as a part of its general corporate assets. Similar terms, restrictions and exemptions, for the benefit of any payee other than the purchaser, may be included by any such company in any annuity contract or any agreement issued in connection therewith or supplemental thereto. When any foreign or alien life insurance company doing business in Connecticut holds the proceeds of a life insurance policy or annuity contract under any trust or other agreement consistent with its charter or the laws of its domicile, beneficiaries of such trust or other agreement shall be entitled to exemptions from claims of creditors as hereinbefore provided to the same extent as if the trust or other agreement were entered into with a domestic life insurance company.

Delaware

Life Insurance:

Proceeds and avails of a life insurance policy are exempt.

Delaware Code – Section 2725 – Exemption of proceeds, life insurance

(a) If a policy of insurance, whether heretofore or hereafter issued, is effected by any person on his/her own life, or on another life, in favor of a person other than himself/herself, or, except in cases of transfer with intent to defraud creditors, if a policy of life insurance is assigned or in any way made payable to any such person, the lawful beneficiary or assignee thereof, other than the insured or the person so effecting such insurance or executors or administrators of such insured or the person so effecting such insurance, shall be entitled to its proceeds and avails against the creditors and representatives of the insured and of the person effecting the same, whether or not the right to change the beneficiary is reserved or permitted and whether or not the policy is made payable to the person whose life is insured if the beneficiary or assignee shall predecease such person, and such proceeds and avails shall be exempt from all liability for any debt of the beneficiary existing at the time the policy is made available for his/her use, provided, that subject to the statute of limitations, the amount of any premiums for such insurance paid with intent to defraud creditors, with interest thereon, shall inure to their benefit from the proceeds of the policy. However, the insurer issuing the policy shall be discharged of all liability thereon by payment of its proceeds in accordance with its terms, unless, before such payment, the insurer shall have received written notice at its home office, by or in behalf of a creditor, of a claim to recover for transfer made or premiums paid with intent to defraud creditors, with specification of the amount claimed along with such facts as will assist the insurer to ascertain the particular policy.

(b) For the purposes of subsection (a) above, a policy shall also be deemed to be payable to a person other than the insured if and to the extent that a facility-of-payment clause or similar clause in the policy permits the insurer to discharge its obligation after the death of the insured.

Annuity Contract:

Monthly payments of up to $350 are exempt.

Delaware Code – Section 2728 – Annuity contracts; Assignability of rights

(a) The benefits, rights, privileges and options which under any annuity contract heretofore or hereafter issued are due or prospectively due the annuitant shall not be subject to execution nor shall the annuitant be compelled to exercise any such rights, powers or options nor shall creditors be allowed to interfere with or terminate the contract, except:

(1) As to amounts paid for or as premium on any such annuity with intent to defraud creditors, with interest thereon, and of which the creditor has given the insurer written notice at its home office prior to the making of the payment to the annuitant out of which the creditor seeks to recover. Any

such notice shall specify the amount claimed or such facts as will enable the insurer to ascertain such amount and shall set forth such facts as will enable the insurer to ascertain the annuity contract, the annuitant and the payment sought to be avoided on the ground of fraud.

(2) The total exemption of benefits presently due and payable to any annuitant periodically or at stated times under all annuity contracts under which he/she is an annuitant shall not at any time exceed $350 per month for the length of time represented by such installments and that such periodic payments in excess of $350 per month shall be subject to garnishee execution to the same extent as are wages and salaries.

(3) If the total benefits presently due and payable to any annuitant under all annuity contracts under which he/she is an annuitant, shall at any time exceed payment at the rate of $350 per month, then the court may order such annuitant to pay to a judgment creditor or apply on the judgment, in installments, such portion of such excess benefits as to the court may appear just and proper, after due regard for the reasonable requirements of the judgment debtor and his/her family, if dependent upon him/her, as well as any payments required to be made by the annuitant to other creditors under prior court orders.

Florida

Life Insurance and Annuity Contract:

Unless the policy indicates otherwise, the proceeds are exempt provided they are not payable to insured or the insured's estate.

The cash value of life insurance policies and annuities are exempt if created to benefit someone other than the insured.

Florida Statute – Sections 222.13 and 222.14

222.13   Life insurance policies; disposition of proceeds.

(1)   Whenever any person residing in the state shall die leaving insurance on his or her life, the said insurance shall inure exclusively to the benefit of the person for whose use and benefit such insurance is designated in the policy, and the proceeds thereof shall be exempt from the claims of creditors of the insured unless the insurance policy or a valid assignment thereof provides otherwise. Notwithstanding the foregoing, whenever the insurance, by designation or otherwise, is payable to the insured or to the insured's estate or to his or her executors, administrators, or assigns, the insurance proceeds shall become a part of the insured's estate for all purposes and shall be administered by the personal representative of the estate of the insured in accordance with the probate laws of the state in like manner as other assets of the insured's estate.

222.14   Exemption of cash surrender value of life insurance policies and annuity contracts from legal process. The cash surrender values of life insurance policies issued upon the lives of citizens or residents of the state and the proceeds of annuity contracts issued to citizens or residents of the state, upon whatever form, shall not in any case be liable to attachment, garnishment or legal process in favor of any creditor of the person whose life is so insured or of any creditor of the person who is the beneficiary of such annuity contract, unless the insurance policy or annuity contract was effected for the benefit of such creditor.

Georgia

Life Insurance and Annuity Contract

Cash surrender value and proceeds of life insurance policies and annuity contracts are not liable to attachment, garnishment, or legal process in favor of creditors.

Georgia Code Annotated – Section 33-25-11 and 33-25-11(c) – Cash surrender value and proceeds of life insurance

33-25-11 – Cash surrender value and proceeds of life insurance policies and annuity contracts not liable to attachment, garnishment, or legal process in favor of creditors; proceeds payable to insured's estate, executor, administrator, or assign to become part of insured's estate

(c) The cash surrender values of life insurance policies issued upon the lives of citizens or residents of this state, upon whatever form, shall not in any case be liable to attachment, garnishment, or legal process in favor of any creditor of the person whose life is so insured unless the insurance policy was assigned to or was effected for the benefit of such creditor or unless the purchase, sale, or transfer of the policy is made with the intent to defraud creditors.

Georgia Code Annotated – Section 33-28-7– Cash surrender value and proceeds of life insurance

33-28-7 – If an annuity, reversionary annuity, or pure endowment contract shall be effected by any person, based on his own life or on another life, payable to a person other than himself, the lawful beneficiary or assignee of the contract, other than the person effecting the contract or his executors or administrators, shall be entitled to its proceeds and avails against the creditors and representatives of the person effecting the contract to the same extent and under the same conditions provided with reference to the proceeds and avails of insurance policies in Code Section 33-25-11.

Hawaii

Life Insurance & Annuity Contract:

Life insurance and annuity contract proceeds payable to spouse, child, parent or other dependent of the insured are exempt.

Group life insurance policies are exempt.

Hawaii Revised Statutes – §431:10-232 – Exemption of proceeds; life, endowment and annuity.

(a) All proceeds payable because of the death of the insured and the aggregate net cash value of any or all life and endowment policies and annuity contracts payable to a spouse of the insured, or to a child, parent or other person dependent upon the insured, whether the power to change the beneficiary is reserved to the insured or not, and whether the insured or the insured›s estate is a contingent beneficiary or not, shall be exempt from execution, attachment, garnishment, or other process, for the debts or liabilities of the insured incurred subsequent to May 19, 1939, except as to premiums paid in fraud of creditors within the period limited by law for the recovery of such payments.

(b) When the terms of any life or endowment policy or annuity contract require that the proceeds thereof be retained by the insurer upon the death of the insured, or other maturity of the policy or contract, for payment to any beneficiary other than the insured in accordance with a settlement plan selected by the insured, the beneficiary shall have no right or power, nor shall the beneficiary be permitted by any insurer, to commute, encumber, assign, or otherwise anticipate the beneficiary›s interests under the plan if the right or power is expressly denied the beneficiary by the terms of the contract or policy. If the beneficiary under the settlement plan is or was the spouse of the insured, or a child, parent or other person dependent upon the insured, the beneficiary›s interests thereunder, in any case, shall be exempt from execution, attachment, garnishment, or other process for the beneficiary›s debts or liabilities incurred after December 31, 1955.

Hawaii Revised Statutes – 431:10-233 – Exemption of proceeds; group life.

(a) A policy of group life insurance or the proceeds thereof payable to the individual insured or to the beneficiary thereunder, shall not be liable, either before or after payment, to be applied to any legal or equitable process to pay any liability of any person having a right under the policy. The proceeds of the policy, when not made payable to a named beneficiary or to a third person pursuant to a facility-of-payment clause, shall not constitute a part of the estate of the individual insured for the payment of the insured's debts.

Idaho

Life Insurance:

The proceeds and avails of life insurance policies are exempt. If the policy makes an agreement with the insurer the proceeds of any unmatured life insurance policy may be held by the insurer against the creditors of the beneficiaries of the policy who are not exempt.

Group life and disability policies are exempt.

Idaho Statutes – Section 41-1833 – Exemption of Proceeds – Life Insurance

(1) If a policy of insurance, whether heretofore or hereafter issued, is effected by any person on his own life, or on another life, in favor of a person other than himself, or, except in cases of transfer with intent to defraud creditors, if a policy of life insurance is assigned or in any way made payable to any such person, the lawful beneficiary or assignee thereof, other than the insured or the person so effecting such insurance or executors or administrators of such insured or the person so effecting such insurance, shall be entitled to its proceeds and avails against the creditors and representatives of the insured and of the person effecting the same, whether or not the right to change the beneficiary is reserved or permitted, and whether or not the policy is made payable to the person whose life is insured if the beneficiary or assignee shall predecease such person, and such proceeds and avails shall be exempt from all liability for any debt of the beneficiary existing at the time the policy is made available for his use: provided, that subject to the statute of limitations, the amount of any premiums for such insurance paid with intent to defraud creditors, with interest thereon, shall inure to their benefit from the proceeds of the policy; but the insurer issuing the policy shall be discharged of all liability thereon by payment of its proceeds in accordance with its terms, unless, before such payment, the insurer shall have received written notice at its home office, by or in behalf of a creditor, of a claim to recover for transfer made or premiums paid with intent to defraud creditors, with specification of the amount claimed.

(2) For the purposes of subsection (1) above, a policy shall also be deemed to be payable to a person other than the insured if and to the extent that a facility-of-payment clause or similar clause in the policy permits the insurer to discharge its obligation after the death of the individual insured by paying the death benefits to a person as permitted by such clause.

Idaho Statutes – Section 41-1930 – Policy Settlements

Any life insurer shall have the power to hold under agreement the proceeds of any policy issued by it, upon such terms and restrictions as to revocation by the policyholder and control by beneficiaries, and with such exemptions from the claims of creditors of beneficiaries other than the policyholder as set forth in the policy or as agreed to in writing by the insurer and the policyholder. Upon maturity of a policy, in the event the policyholder has made no such agreement, the insurer shall have the power to hold the proceeds of the policy under an agreement with the beneficiaries. The insurer shall not be required to segregate the funds so held but may hold them as part of its general assets.

Idaho Statutes – Section 41-1835 – Exemptions of Proceeds – Group Insurance

(1) A policy of group life insurance or group disability insurance or the proceeds thereof payable to the individual insured or to the beneficiary thereunder, shall not be liable, either before or after payment, to be applied by any legal or equitable process to pay any debt or liability of such insured individual or his beneficiary or of any other person having a right under the policy. The proceeds thereof, when not made payable to a named beneficiary or to a third person pursuant to a facility-of-payment clause, shall not constitute a part of the estate of the individual insured for the payment of his debts.

(2) This section shall not apply to group insurance issued pursuant to this code to a creditor covering his debtors, to the extent that such proceeds are applied to payment of the obligation for the purpose of which the insurance was so issued.

Annuity Contract:

Any benefits, rights, privileges and options under an annuity contract are exempt up to $1,250 per month.

Idaho Statutes – Section 41-1836 – Exemption of Proceeds – Annuity Contacts – Assignability of Rights

(1) The benefits, rights, privileges and options which under any annuity contract heretofore or hereafter issued are due or prospectively due the annuitant, shall not be subject to execution nor shall the annuitant be compelled to exercise any such rights, powers, or options, nor shall creditors be allowed to interfere with or terminate the contract, except:

(a) As to amounts paid for or as premium on any such annuity with intent to defraud creditors, with interest thereon, and of which the creditor has given the insurer written notice at its home office prior to the making of the payments to the annuitant out of which the creditor seeks to recover. Any such notice shall specify the amount claimed or such facts as will enable the insurer to ascertain such amount, and shall set forth such facts as will enable the insurer to ascertain the annuity contract, the annuitant and the payments sought to be avoided on the ground of fraud.

(b) The total exemption of benefits presently due and payable to any annuitant periodically or at stated times under all annuity contracts under which he is an annuitant, shall not at any time exceed one thousand two hundred fifty dollars ($1,250) per month for the length of time represented by such installments, and that such periodic payments in excess of one thousand two hundred fifty dollars ($1,250) per month shall be subject to garnishee execution to the same extent as are wages and salaries.

(c) If the total benefits presently due and payable to any annuitant under all annuity contracts under which he is an annuitant, shall at any time exceed payment at the rate of one thousand two hundred fifty dollars ($1,250) per month, then the court may order such annuitant to pay to a judgment creditor or apply on the judgment, in installments, such portion of such excess benefits as to the court may appear just and proper, after due regard for the reasonable requirements of the judgment debtor and his family, if dependent upon him, as well as any payments required to be made by the annuitant to other creditors under prior court orders.

Illinois

Life Insurance:

The death proceeds and cash value of life insurance, endowment policies payable to spouse, child, parent or other dependent of the insured are exempt.

Group life insurance proceeds are exempt.

Illinois Complied Statutes – Section 12-1001(g) – Personal Property Exempt

The following personal property, owned by the debtor, is exempt from judgment, attachment, or distress for rent:

(g) All proceeds payable because of the death of the insured and the aggregate net cash value of any or all life insurance and endowment policies and annuity contracts payable to a wife or husband of the insured, or to a child, parent, or other person dependent upon the insured, or to a revocable or irrevocable trust which names the wife or husband of the insured or which names a child, parent, or other person dependent upon the insured as the primary beneficiary of the trust, whether the power to change the beneficiary is reserved to the insured or not and whether the insured or the insured's estate is a contingent beneficiary or not.

Annuity Contract:

The death proceeds and cash value of life insurance, endowment policies payable to spouse, child, parent or other dependent of the insured are exempt.

Illinois Compiled Statutes – Section 238(a)- Exemption

Sec. 238. Exemption.

All proceeds payable because of the death of the insured and the aggregate net cash value of any or all life and endowment policies and annuity contracts payable to a wife or husband of the insured, or to a child, parent or other person dependent upon the insured, whether the power to change the beneficiary is reserved to the insured or not, and whether the insured or his estate is a contingent beneficiary or not, shall be exempt from execution, attachment, garnishment or other process, for the debts or liabilities of the insured incurred subsequent to the effective date of this Code, except as to premiums paid in fraud of creditors within the period limited by law for the recovery thereof.

Indiana

Life Insurance & Annuity Contract:

Policy proceeds are exempt if payments are directed to the insured's spouse, children or other relative dependent.

Life insurance and annuity contracts are exempt unless there is a provision stating otherwise.

Premiums paid within 1 year of bankruptcy or with intent to defraud creditors are protected.

Indiana Code Annotated – Section 27-2-5-1 – Spendthrift laws; exemption from judicial process

Sec. 1. (a) As used in this section, "premium" includes any deposit or contribution.

(b) No person entitled to receive benefits under a life insurance or life annuity contract, or under a written agreement supplemental thereto, issued by domestic life insurance company, shall be permitted to commute, anticipate, encumber, alienate, or assign such benefits, if the right to do so is expressly prohibited or withheld by a provision contained in such contract or supplemental agreement. And if such contract, policy, or supplemental agreement so provides, such benefits, except when payable to the person who provided the consideration for such contract, shall not be subject to such persons' debts, contracts, or engagements, nor to any judicial process to levy upon or attach the same for payment thereof.

(c) A premium paid for an individual life insurance policy that names as a beneficiary, or is legally assigned to, a spouse, child, or relative who is dependent upon the policy owner is not exempt from the claims of the creditors of the policy owner if the premium is paid:

> (1) not more than one (1) year before the date of the filing of a voluntary or involuntary petition by; or

> (2) to defraud the creditors of; the policy owner.

Indiana Code Annotated – Section 27-1-12-14 Designation of beneficiary; change of beneficiary; eligible beneficiaries; exemption of policy proceeds from claims of creditors

Sec. 14. (a) As used in this section, "premium" includes any deposit or contribution.

(b) As used in this section, «proceeds or avails» means death benefits, cash surrender and loan values, premiums waived, and dividends whether used in reduction of the premiums or in whatsoever manner used or applied, excepting only where the debtor has, subsequent to the issuance of the policy, actually elected to receive the dividends in cash.

(c) Any person whose life is insured by any life insurance company may name as his payee or beneficiary any person or persons, natural or artificial, with or without an insurable interest, or his estate. A designation at the option of the policyowner may be made either revocable or irrevocable, and the option elected shall be set out in and shall be made a part of the application for the certificate or policy of insurance. When the right of revocation has been reserved, the person whose life is insured, subject to any existing assignment of the policy, may at any time designate a new payee or beneficiary, with or without reserving the right of revocation, by filing written notice thereof at the home office of the corporation, accompanied by the policy for suitable endorsement thereon.

(d) Any person may effect an insurance on his life, for any definite period of time, or for the term of his natural life, to inure to the sole benefit of the spouse and children, or of either, or other relative or relatives dependent upon such person or any creditor or creditors as he may cause to be appointed and provided in the policy.

(e) Except as provided in subsection (g), all policies of life insurance upon the life of any person, which name as beneficiary, or are bona fide assigned to, the spouse, children, or any relative dependent upon such person, or any creditor, shall be held, subject to change of beneficiary from time to time, if desired, for the benefit of such spouse, children, other relative or creditor, free and clear from all claims of the creditors of such insured person or of the person›s spouse; and the proceeds or avails of all such life insurance shall be exempt from all liabilities from any debt or debts of such insured person or of the person›s spouse.

(f) A premium paid for an individual life insurance policy that names as a beneficiary, or is legally assigned to, a spouse, child, or relative who is dependent upon the policy owner is not exempt from the claims of the creditors of the policy owner if the premium is paid: (1) not more than one (1) year before the date of the filing of a voluntary or involuntary bankruptcy petition by; or (2) to defraud the creditors of; the policy owner.

Iowa

Life Insurance:

Interest in accrued dividend or interest, or loan or cash surrender value for the benefit of a spouse, child or dependent are exempt provided the interest acquired shall not exceed $10,000 in the previous two years.

Up to $15,000 is exempt from a matured life insurance policy payable to a spouse, child or dependent are exempt from the beneficiary's creditors.

Iowa Code – Section 627.6(6) – General Exemptions

A debtor who is a resident of this state may hold exempt from execution the following property:

6. The interest of an individual in any accrued dividend or interest, loan or cash surrender value of, or any other interest in life insurance policy owned by the individual if the beneficiary of the policy is the individual's spouse, child, or dependent. However the amount of the exemption shall not exceed ten thousand dollars in the aggregate of any interest or value in insurance acquired within two years of the date execution is issued or exemptions are claimed, or for additions within the same time period to a prior existing policy which additions are in excess of the amount necessary to fund the amount of face value coverage of the policies for the two-year period. For purposes of this paragraph, acquisitions shall not include such interest in new policies used to replace prior policies to the extent of any accrued dividend or interest, loan or cash surrender value of, or any other interest in the prior policies at the time of their cancellation.

Annuity Contract:

Proceeds wholly exempt except for payments resulting from excessive contributions within the prior year.

Iowa Code – Section 627.6(8)(e) – General Exemptions

A debtor who is a resident of this state may hold exempt from execution the following property:

8. The debtor's rights in:

> *e.* A payment or a portion of a payment under a pension, annuity, or similar plan or contract on account of illness, disability, death, age, or length of service, unless the payment or a portion of the payment results from contributions to the

plan or contract by the debtor within one year prior to the filing of a bankruptcy petition, which contributions are above the normal and customary contributions under the plan or contract, in which case the portion of the payment attributable to the contributions above the normal and customary rate is not exempt.

Kansas

Life Insurance:

The policy and its reserves are exempt from creditors unless purchased within the previous year.

Kansas Statutes Annotated – Section 40-414(a)(b) – Exemption of interests in policies; exceptions.

(a) If a life insurance company or fraternal benefit society issues any policy of insurance or beneficiary certificates upon the life of an individual and payable at the death of the insured, or in any given number of years, to any person or persons having an insurable interest in the life of the insured, the policy and its reserves, or their present value, shall inure to the sole and separate use and benefit of the beneficiaries named in the policy and shall be free from:

(1) The claims of the insured or the insured›s creditors and representatives;

(2) the claims of any policyholder or the policyholder›s creditors and representatives, subject to the provisions of subsection (b);

(3) all taxes, subject to the provisions of subsection (d); and

(4) the claims and judgments of the creditors and representatives of any person named as beneficiary in the policy of insurance.

(b) The nonforfeiture value of a life insurance policy shall not be exempt from:

(1) Claims of the creditors of a policyholder who files a bankruptcy petition under 11 U.S.C. § 101 et seq. on or within one year after the date the policy is issued; or

(2) the claim of any creditor of a policyholder if execution on judgment for the claim is issued on or within one year after the date that the policy is issued.

Annuity Contract:

Annuities that qualify under statute are exempt from creditors.

Kansas Statutes Annotated – Section 60-2313(a)(1) – Exemptions from legal process.

(a) Except to the extent otherwise provided by law, every person residing in this state shall have exempt from seizure and sale upon any attachment, execution or other process issued from any court in this state:

(1) Any pension, annuity, retirement, disability, death or other benefit exempt from process pursuant to K.S.A. 12-111a, 12-5005, 13-1246a, 13-14,102, 13-14a10, 14-10a10, 20-2618, 72-1768, 72-5526, 74-4923, 74-4978g, 74-49,105 or 74-49,106, and amendments thereto.

Kentucky

Life Insurance:

Proceeds and avails of a life insurance policy are exempt.

Kentucky Revised Statutes Annotated – Section 304.14 – 300 – Exemptions of Proceeds, life insurance

(1) If a policy of insurance whether heretofore or hereafter issued, is effected by any person on his own life, or on another life, in favor of a person other than himself, or, except in cases of transfer with intent to defraud creditors, if a policy of life insurance is assigned or

in any way made payable to any such person, the lawful beneficiary or assignee thereof, other than the insured or the person so effecting such insurance or executors or administrators of such insured or the person so effecting such insurance, shall be entitled to its proceeds and avails against the creditors and representatives of the insured and of the person effecting the same, whether or not the right to change the beneficiary is reserved or permitted and whether or not the policy is made payable to the person whose life is insured if the beneficiary or assignee shall predecease such person, and such proceeds and avails shall be exempt from all liability for any debt of the beneficiary existing at the time the policy is made available for his use: provided, that subject to the statute of limitations, the amount of any premiums for such insurance paid with intent to defraud creditors, with interest thereon, shall inure to their benefit from the proceeds of the policy; but the insurer issuing the policy shall be discharged of all liability thereon by payment of its proceeds in accordance with its terms, unless, before such payment, the insurer shall have received written notice at its principal office, by or in behalf of a creditor, of a claim to recover for transfer made or premiums paid with intent to defraud creditors, with specification of the amount claimed.

(2) For the purposes of subsection (1) of this section, a policy shall also be deemed to be payable to a person other than the insured if and to the extent that a facility-of-payment clause or similar clause in the policy permits the insurer to discharge its obligation after the death of the individual insured by paying the death benefits to a person as permitted by such clause.

Annuity Contract:

Benefits, rights, privileges, and options under an annuity contract are exempt up to $350 per month.

Kentucky Revised Statutes Annotated – Section 304.14 – 330 – Exemptions of Proceeds, annuity contracts

(1) The benefits, rights, privileges and options which under any annuity contract heretofore or hereafter issued are due or

prospectively due the annuitant, shall not be subject to execution nor shall the annuitant be compelled to exercise any such rights, powers, or options, nor shall creditors be allowed to interfere with or terminate the contract, except:

(a) As to amounts paid for or as premium on any such annuity with intent to defraud creditors, with interest thereon, and of which the creditor has given the insurer written notice at its principal office prior to the making of the payment to the annuitant out of which the creditor seeks to recover. Any such notice shall specify the amount claimed or such facts as will enable the insurer to ascertain such amount, and shall set forth such facts as will enable the insurer to ascertain the annuity contract, the annuitant and the payment sought to be avoided on the ground of fraud.

(b) The total exemption of benefits presently due and payable to any annuitant periodically or at stated times under all annuity contracts under which he is an annuitant, shall not at any time exceed $350 per month for the length of time represented by such installments, and that such periodic payments in excess of $350 per month shall be subject to garnishee execution to the same extent as are wages and salaries.

(c) If the total benefits presently due and payable to any annuitant under all annuity contracts under which he is an annuitant, shall at any time exceed payment at the rate of $350 per month, then the court may order such annuitant to pay to a judgment creditor or apply on the judgment, in installments, such portion of such excess benefits as to the court may appear just and proper, after due regard for the reasonable requirements of the judgment debtor and his family, if dependent upon him, as well as any payments required to be made by the annuitant to other creditors under prior court orders.

Louisiana

Life Insurance and Annuity Contract:

Proceeds and avails of a life insurance policy are exempt.

In a bankruptcy proceeding cash surrender and loan values exceeding $35,000 are not exempt if the policy was issued within nine months of filing.

Louisiana Revised Statutes – Section 22:912 – Exemption of proceeds; life, endowment, annuity

A. (1) The lawful beneficiary, assignee, or payee, including the insured's estate, of a life insurance policy or endowment policy, shall be entitled to the proceeds and avails of the policy against the creditors and representatives of the insured and of the person effecting the policy or the estate of either, and against the heirs and legatees of either person, and such proceeds and avails shall also be exempt from all liability for any debt of the beneficiary, payee, or assignee or estate, existing at the time the proceeds or avails are made available for his own use. For purposes of this Subsection, the proceeds and avails of the policy include the cash surrender value of the policy.

(2) The exemption authorized in Paragraph (1) of this Subsection from seizure under any writ, mandate, or process issued by any court of competent jurisdiction, including any bankruptcy proceedings, shall not apply to that portion of the cash surrender value, or loan value of any life insurance policy, endowment policy, or annuity contract payable upon surrender during the lifetime of the insured or annuitant which exceeds the sum of thirty-five thousand dollars if such policy or contract was issued within nine months of issuance of such writ, mandate, or process or the filing of a voluntary or involuntary bankruptcy proceeding under the United States Code. However, an insurer shall be liable only for such amounts that exceed the thirty-five thousand dollar exemption which are in the insurer's possession at the time the insurer

receives, at its home office, written notice by or on behalf of a creditor of claims being made against such value or interest with specification of the amount claimed. The insurer shall have no obligation to determine the validity or the accuracy of the amount of the claim and shall be relieved of further liability of any kind with respect to the monies paid upon request of a creditor. An insurer shall be entitled to be paid by preference and priority over the claim of any seizing creditor the balance of any bona fide loan to the insured or owner which is secured by such interest or value in the policy or contract.

Maine

Life Insurance and Annuity Contract:

Except in cases with an intent to defraud creditors the proceeds and avails of contracts for life, endowment, and annuity contracts are exempt.

For dividends, interest or loans value of any unmatured life insurance contract the debtor's aggregate interest cannot exceed $4,000.

Benefits, rights, privileges and options under an annuity contract are exempt up to $450 per month.

Maine Revised Statutes Annotated – Title 24 – A Section 2428 – Exemptions of Proceeds – Life Endowment, Annuity, Accident Contracts

1. Certain policies of insurance shall be exempt from claims of creditors, and the rights of beneficiaries and assignees thereof shall be protected, as set forth.

2. Except in cases of transfers with intent to defraud creditors, if a contract of life, endowment, annuity or accident insurance, whether heretofore or hereafter issued, is effected by any person on his own life or on another life, in favor of a person other than himself or is assigned or in any way made payable to any other

person, the lawful beneficiary or assignee thereof, other than the insured or the person so effecting such contract of insurance or executors or administrators of such insured or of the person so effecting such contract of insurance, shall be entitled to its proceeds and avails against the creditors and representatives of the insured and of the person effecting the same, whether or not the right to change the beneficiary is reserved or permitted and whether or not the contract of insurance is made payable to the person whose life is insured or to the executor or administrator of such person if the beneficiary or assignee shall predecease such person, and such proceeds and avails shall be exempt from all liability for any debt of the beneficiary existing at the time the proceeds and avails is made available for his use. Subject to the statutes of limitations, the amount of any premiums for such contract of insurance paid with intent to defraud creditors, with interest thereon, shall inure to the benefit of the creditors from the proceeds of the contract of insurance; but the insurer issuing the contract shall be discharged of all liability thereon by payment of its proceeds in accordance with its terms, unless before such payment the insurer shall have received written notice, by or in behalf of a creditor with specifications of the amount claimed along with such facts as will assist the insurer to ascertain the particular policy, of a claim to recover for transfer made or premiums paid with intent to defraud creditors, and unless such insurer shall have been served with trustee process for the cash surrender value of any such contract of insurance as required by law prior to making payment of the proceeds in accordance with the terms of the contract of insurance.

Maine Revised Statutes Annotated – Title 24 – A Section 2431 – Exemption of proceeds, individual annuity contracts; assignability of rights

1. The benefits, rights, privileges and options which under any individual annuity contract heretofore or hereafter issued are due or prospectively due the annuitant, shall not be subject to execution nor shall the annuitant be compelled to exercise any such rights, powers, or options, nor shall creditors be allowed to interfere with or terminate the contract, except:

A. As to amounts paid for or as premium on any such annuity with intent to defraud creditors, with interest thereon, and of which the creditor has given the insurer written notice received at its home office prior to the making of the payment to the annuitant out of which the creditor seeks to recover. Any such notice shall specify the amount claimed or such facts as will enable the insurer to ascertain such amount, and shall set forth such facts as will enable the insurer to ascertain the annuity contract, the annuitant and the payment sought to be avoided on the ground of fraud.

B. The total exemption of benefits presently due and payable to any annuitant periodically or at stated times under all annuity contracts under which he is an annuitant, shall not at any time exceed $450 per month for the length of time represented by such installments, and that such periodic payments in excess of $450 per month shall be subject to garnishee execution to the same extent as are wages and salaries.

C. If the total benefits presently due and payable to any annuitant under all annuity contracts under which he is an annuitant, shall at any time exceed payment at the rate of $450 per month, then the court may order such annuitant to pay to a judgment creditor or apply on the judgment, in installments, such portion of such excess benefits as to the court may appear just and proper, after due regard for the reasonable requirements of the judgment debtor and his family, if dependent upon him, as well as any payments required to be made by the annuitant to other creditors under prior court orders.

2. If the contract so provides, the benefits, rights, privileges or options accruing under such contract to a beneficiary or assignee shall not be transferable nor subject to commutation, and if the benefits are payable periodically or at stated times, the same exemptions and exceptions contained herein for the annuitant, shall apply with respect to such beneficiary or assignee.

Maine Revised Statutes Annotated – Title 24 – A Section 4422(10) & (11) – Exempt Property

The following property is exempt from attachment and execution, except to the extent that it has been fraudulently conveyed by the debtor.

10. Life insurance contract. Any unmatured life insurance contract owned by the debtor, other than a credit life insurance contract.

11. Life insurance dividends, interest and loan value. The debtor's aggregate interest, not to exceed in value $4,000 less any amount of property of the estate transferred in the manner specified in the United States Code, Title 11, Section 542(d), in any accrued dividend or interest under, or loan value of, any unmatured life insurance contract owned by the debtor under which the insured is the debtor or an individual of whom the debtor is dependent.

Maryland

Life Insurance and Annuity Contract:

The proceeds are exempt if payable to the spouse, child, or dependent relative of the insured. The proceeds include the death benefit, cash surrender and loan values, premiums waived and dividends.

Maryland Code Annotated – Section 16-111

(a) The proceeds of a policy of life insurance or under an annuity contract on the life of an individual made for the benefit of or assigned to the spouse, child, or dependent relative of the individual are exempt from all claims of the creditors of the individual arising out of or based on an obligation created after June 1, 1945, whether or not the right to change the named beneficiary is reserved or allowed to the individual.

(b) For purposes of this section, proceeds include death benefits, cash surrender and loan values, premiums waived, and dividends, whether used to reduce the premiums or used or applied in any other manner, except if the debtor has, after issuance of the policy, elected to receive the dividends in cash.

(c) This section does not prohibit a creditor from collecting a debt out of the proceeds of a life insurance policy pledged by the insured as security for the debt.

(d) A change of beneficiary, assignment, or other transfer is valid except for transfer with actual intent to hinder, delay, or defraud creditors.

Massachusetts

Life Insurance:

Life insurance proceeds are exempt.

Life insurance proceeds for a married woman are exempt if the proceeds are for her benefit and that of her children.

Massachusetts General Laws Chapter 175 – Section 119A – Insurance benefits; protection of beneficiaries

If, under the terms of any annuity contract or policy of life insurance, or under any written agreement supplemental thereto, issued by any life company, the proceeds are retained by such company at maturity or otherwise, no person entitled to any part of such proceeds, or any installment of interest due or to become due thereon, shall be permitted to commute, anticipate, encumber, alienate or assign the same, or any part thereof, if such permission is expressly withheld by the terms of such contract, policy or supplemental agreement; and if such contract, policy or supplemental agreement so provides, no payments of interest or of principal shall be in any way subject to such person's debts, contracts or engagements, nor to any judicial processes to levy upon or attach the same for payment thereof. No such company shall be required to segregate such funds but may hold them as a part of its general corporate funds.

Massachusetts General Laws Chapter 175 – Section 125 – Creditors or beneficiaries; rights

If a policy of life or endowment insurance is effected by any person on his own life or on another life, in favor of a person other than himself having an insurable interest therein, the lawful beneficiary thereof, other than himself or his legal representatives, shall be entitled to its proceeds against the creditors and representatives of the person effecting the same, whether or not the right to change the named beneficiary is reserved by or permitted to such person; provided, that, subject to the statute of limitations, the amount of any premiums for said insurance paid in fraud of creditors, with interest thereon, shall enure to their benefit from the proceeds of the policy; but the company issuing the policy shall be discharged of all liability thereon by payment of its proceeds in accordance with its terms, unless before such payment the company shall have written notice, by or on behalf of a creditor, of a claim to recover for certain premiums paid in fraud of creditors, with specification of the amount claimed. No court, and no trustee or assignee for the benefit of creditors, shall elect for the person effecting such insurance to exercise such right to change the named beneficiary.

Massachusetts General Laws Chapter 175 – Section 126 – Married woman; beneficiary under insurance contract

Every policy of life or endowment insurance made payable to or for the benefit of a married woman, or after its issue assigned, transferred or in any way made payable to a married woman, or to any person in trust for her or for her benefit, whether procured by herself, her husband or by any other person, and whether the assignment or transfer is made by her husband or by any other person, and whether or not the right to change the named beneficiary is reserved by or permitted to the person effecting such insurance, shall enure to her separate use and benefit, and to that of her children, subject to the provisions of section one hundred and twenty-five relative to premiums paid in fraud of creditors and to sections one hundred and forty-four to one hundred and forty-six, inclusive. No court, and no trustee or assignee for the benefit of creditors, shall elect for the person effecting such insurance to exercise such right to change the named beneficiary.

Annuity Contract:

Group annuity contract proceeds and benefits are exempt.

Massachusetts General Laws Chapter 175 – Section 132C – Group annuity contract; exemption from process; exception

No group annuity contract, nor the proceeds or benefits thereof, shall be liable, either before or after payment, to be seized, taken, appropriated or applied by any legal or equitable process or operation of law to pay any debt or liabilities of the annuitant or his beneficiary or any other person having any right thereunder; nor shall the benefits or proceeds upon the death of an annuitant, when not made payable to a beneficiary, constitute a part of the estate of the annuitant for the payment of his debts.

Nothing in this section shall prevent an annuitant's benefits from being seized, taken, appropriated, assigned, or applied by any legal or equitable process or operation of law to satisfy a support order under chapter two hundred and eight, two hundred and nine, or two hundred and seventy-three.

Michigan

Life Insurance and Annuity Contract:

Life insurance and annuity contract proceeds are exempt.

Michigan Complied Laws – Section 500.2207 – Insurance interest; personal insurance; rights of beneficiaries, creditors

(1) It shall be lawful for any husband to insure his life for the benefit of his wife, and for any father to insure his life for the

benefit of his children, or of any one or more of them; and in case that any money shall become payable under the insurance, the same shall be payable to the person or persons for whose benefit the insurance was procured, his, her or their representatives or assigns, for his, her or their own use and benefit, free from all claims of the representatives of such husband or father, or of any of his creditors; and any married woman, either in her own name or in the name of any third person as her trustee, may cause to be insured the life of her husband, or of any other person, for any definite period, or for the term of life, and the moneys that may become payable on the contract of insurance, shall be payable to her, her representatives or assigns, free from the claims of the representatives of the husband, or of such other person insured, or of any of his creditors; and in any contract of insurance, it shall be lawful to provide that on the decease of the person or persons for whose benefit it is obtained, before the sum insured shall become payable, the benefit thereof shall accrue to any other person or persons designated; and such other person or persons shall, on the happening of such contingency, succeed to all the rights and benefits of the deceased beneficiary or beneficiaries of the policy of insurance, notwithstanding he, she or they may not at the time have any such insurable interest as would have enabled him, her or them to obtain a new insurance; and the proceeds of any policy of life or endowment insurance, which is payable to the wife, husband or children of the insured or to a trustee for the benefit of the wife, husband or children of the insured, including the cash value thereof, shall be exempt from execution or liability to any creditor of the insured; and said exemption shall apply to insurance heretofore or hereafter issued; and shall apply to insurance payable to the above enumerated persons or classes of persons, whether they shall have become entitled thereto as originally designated beneficiaries, by beneficiary designation subsequent to the issuance of the policy, or by assignment (except in case of transfer with intent to defraud creditors).

(2) If a policy of insurance, or contract of annuity (whether heretofore or hereafter issued) is effected by any person on his own life or on another life in favor of a person other than himself, or (except in cases of transfer with intent to defraud creditors) if a

policy of life insurance is assigned or in any way made payable to any such person, the lawful beneficiary or assignee thereof (other than the insured or the person so effecting such insurance, or his executors or administrators) shall be entitled to the proceeds and avails (including the cash value thereof) against the creditors and representatives of the insured and of the person effecting the same, (whether or not the right to change the beneficiary is reserved or permitted and whether or not the policy is made payable in the event that the beneficiary or assignee shall predecease such person, to the person whose life is insured or the person effecting the insurance): Provided, That, subject to the statute of limitations, the amount of any premiums for said insurance paid with intent to defraud creditors, with interest thereon, shall inure to their benefit from the proceeds of the policy: Provided further, That proof that such transfer was made and a particular debt or claim existed at the time of such transfer shall be prima facie evidence of intent to defraud said creditor as to said debt or claim; but the company issuing the policy shall be discharged of all liability thereon by payment of its proceeds in accordance with its terms, unless before such payment the company shall have written notice at its home office, by or in behalf of a creditor of a claim to recover for transfer made or premiums paid with intent to defraud creditors, with specification of the amount claimed.

Michigan Complied Laws – Section 500.4054 – Proceeds of policy; exemption from creditors

(1) Any authorized life insurer shall have power to hold the proceeds of any life or endowment insurance or annuity contract issued by it (a) upon such terms and restrictions as to revocation by the insured and control by beneficiaries; (b) with such exemptions from legal process and the claims of creditors of beneficiaries other than the insured; and (c) upon such other terms and conditions, irrespective of the time and manner of payment of said proceeds, as shall have been agreed to in writing by such insurer and the insured or beneficiary.

(2) Such insurer shall not be required to segregate funds so held but may hold them as a part of its general corporate assets.

(3) Any life or endowment insurance or annuity contract issued by a domestic, foreign or alien insurer may provide that the proceeds thereof or payments thereunder shall not be subject to the claims of creditors of any beneficiary other than the insured or any legal process against any beneficiary other than the insured; and if the said contract so provides, the benefits accruing thereunder to such beneficiary other than the insured shall not be transferable nor subject to commutation or encumbrance, or to process.

Minnesota

Life Insurance and Annuity Contract:

Life insurance and annuity contract proceeds are exempt, when created for the benefit of another.

Funds paid or payable to a surviving spouse or child is limited to $46,000 with an additional $11,500 per dependent.

Unmatured life insurance in which the debtor is the insured is exempt up to $9,200.

Minnesota Statutes – Section 61A.12 – Beneficiaries

1. Proceeds of life policy or annuity, who entitled to. When any insurance is effected in favor of another, the beneficiary shall be entitled to its proceeds against the creditors and representatives of the person effecting the same. All premiums paid for insurance in fraud of creditors, with interest thereon, shall inure to their benefit from the proceeds of the policy, if the company be specifically notified thereof, in writing, before payment.

2. Exemption in favor of family. Every policy made payable to, or for the benefit of, the spouse of the insured, or after its issue assigned to or in trust for a spouse, shall inure to that person's separate use and that of the children of the insured or the insured's spouse, subject to the provisions of this section.

Minnesota Statutes – Section 550.37 – Property Exempt

10. Insurance proceeds. All money received by, or payable to, a surviving spouse or child from insurance payable at the death of a spouse, or parent, not exceeding $46,000. The $46,000 exemption provided by this subdivision shall be increased by $11,500 for each dependent of the surviving spouse or child.

23. Life insurance aggregate interest. The debtor's aggregate interest not to exceed in value $9,200 in any accrued dividend or interest under or loan value of any unmatured life insurance contract owned by the debtor under which the insured is the debtor or an individual of whom the debtor is a dependent.

Mississippi

Life Insurance and Annuity Contract:

Life insurance and annuity contract proceeds are exempt if specified in the policy.

Exemption shall not apply in an unmatured life insurance policy with a cash value in excess of $50,000 as a result of premiums and payments made within twelve months of creditor claim.

Mississippi Code Annotated – Section 83-7-5 – Proceeds of policy not subject to judicial process or assignment while in the hand of company.

If, under the terms of any annuity contract, or policy of life insurance, or under any written agreement supplemental thereto issued by any life insurance company, the proceeds are retained by such company at maturity or otherwise, no person entitled to any part of such proceeds, or any installments of interest due or to become due thereon, shall be permitted to commute, anticipate, encumber, alienate, or assign the same, or any part thereof, if such permission is expressly withheld by the terms of such contract, policy, or supplemental agreement. If such contract, policy, or supplemental agreement so provides, no payment of interest or of principal shall be in any way subject to such person's debts, contracts, or engagements, nor to any judicial processes to levy upon or attach the same for payment thereof. No such company shall be required to segregate such funds, but may hold them as a part of its general corporate funds.

Mississippi Code Annotated – Section 83-3-11 – Proceeds of life insurance policy; named beneficiaries; certain proceeds of policies exempt from liability for debts of person insured.

(1) Except as provided in subsection (2), all proceeds of a life insurance policy including cash surrender and loan values, shall inure to the party or parties named as the beneficiaries thereof, free from all liability for the debts of the person whose life was insured, even though such person paid the premium thereon. In addition, all proceeds, including cash surrender and loan values, of a policy of life insurance owned by or assigned to another, shall inure to the beneficiary or beneficiaries named therein, subject to terms of any assignment, free from all liability for debts of the person whose life was insured.

(2)

    (a) The exemption authorized in Subsection (1) shall not apply to that portion of the cash surrender value or loan value of any life insurance policy which exceeds the sum of Fifty Thousand Dollars ($50,000.00) as a result of premiums paid or premium deposits or other payments made within twelve (12) months of issuance of a writ of seizure, attachment, garnishment or other process or the filing of a voluntary or involuntary bankruptcy proceeding under the United States Code.

    (b) The amount of any premiums for the insurance paid with intent to defraud creditors, with interest thereon, shall inure to the benefit of such creditors from the proceeds of the policy; but the insurer issuing the policy shall be discharged of all liabilities thereon by payment of its proceeds in accordance with its terms, unless before such payment the insurer shall have written notice, by or on behalf of a creditor, of a claim to recover for transfer made or premiums paid with intent to defraud creditors with specification of the amount claimed.

(c) Notwithstanding any other provision to the contrary, a creditor possessing a valid assignment from the policy owner may recover from either the cash surrender value or the proceeds of the life insurance policy the amount secured by the assignment with interest.

Missouri

Life Insurance:

Exemption shall not apply in an unmatured life insurance policy with a cash value in excess of $150,000 as a result of premiums and payments made within twelve months of creditor claim.

Proceeds of a life insurance policy are exempt.

Missouri Revised Statutes – Section 513.430 – Property exempt from attachment

The following property shall be exempt from attachment and execution to the extent of any person's interest therein:

(7) Any one or more unmatured life insurance contracts owned by such person, other than a credit life insurance contract;

(8) The amount of any accrued dividend or interest under, or loan value of, any one or more unmatured life insurance contracts owned by such person under which the insured is such person or an individual of whom such person is a dependent; provided, however, that if proceedings under Title 11 of the United States Code are commenced by or against such person, the amount exempt in such proceedings shall not exceed in value one hundred fifty

thousand dollars in the aggregate less any amount of property of such person transferred by the life insurance company or fraternal benefit society to itself in good faith if such transfer is to pay a premium or to carry out a nonforfeiture insurance option and is required to be so transferred automatically under a life insurance contract with such company or society that was entered into before commencement of such proceedings. No amount of any accrued dividend or interest under, or loan value of, any such life insurance contracts shall be exempt from any claim for child support. Notwithstanding anything to the contrary, no such amount shall be exempt in such proceedings under any such insurance contract which was purchased by such person within one year prior to the commencement of such proceedings;

Missouri Revised Statutes – Section 377.090 – Proceeds not liable for debts.

The money or other benefit, charity, relief or aid to be paid, provided or rendered by any corporation authorized to do business under sections 377.010 to 377.190, shall not be liable to attachment or other process, and shall not be seized, taken, appropriated or applied by any legal or equitable process, nor by operation of law, to pay any debt or liability of a policy or certificate holder, or any beneficiary named in a policy or certificate.

Annuity Contract: No Specific Statute

Montana

Life Insurance:

Life insurance proceeds and cash surrender value are exempt.

Group life insurance proceeds are exempt.

Montana Code Annotated – Section 33-15-511- Exemption from execution of life insurance proceeds.

(1) If a policy of insurance, whether heretofore or hereafter issued, is effected by any person on his own life or on another life in favor of a person other than himself or, except in cases of transfer with intent to defraud creditors, if a policy of life insurance is assigned or in any way made payable to any such person, the lawful beneficiary or assignee thereof, other than the insured or the person so effecting such insurance or executors or administrators of such insured or the person so effecting such insurance, shall be entitled to its proceeds and avails against the creditors and representatives of the insured and of the person effecting the same, whether or not the right to change the beneficiary is reserved or permitted and whether or not the policy is made payable to the person whose life is insured if the beneficiary or assignee shall predecease such person; except that, subject to the statute of limitations, the amount of any premiums for such insurance paid with intent to defraud creditors with interest thereon shall enure to their benefit from the proceeds of the policy, but the insurer issuing the policy shall be discharged of all liability thereof by payment of its proceeds in accordance with its terms, unless before such payment the insurer shall have received written notice at its home office, by or in behalf of a creditor, of a claim to recover for transfer made or premiums paid with intent to defraud creditors, with specifications of the amount so claimed.

(2) For the purposes of subsection (1) above, a policy shall also be deemed to be payable to a person other than the insured if and to the extent that a facility-of-payment clause or similar clause in the policy permits the insurer to discharge its obligation after the death of the individual insured by paying the death benefits to a person as permitted by such clause.

Montana Code Annotated – Section 33-15-512- Exemption from execution of life insurance proceeds of group life – Exception.

(1) A policy of group life insurance or the proceeds thereof payable to the individual insured or to the beneficiary thereunder shall not be liable, either before or after payment, to be applied by any legal or equitable process to pay any debt or liability of such insured individual or his beneficiary or of any other person having a right

under the policy. The proceeds thereof, when not made payable to a named beneficiary or to a third person pursuant to a facility-of-payment clause, shall not constitute a part of the estate of the individual insured for the payment of his debts.

(2) This section shall not apply to group life insurance issued pursuant to parts 10, 11, and 12 of chapter 20 to a creditor covering his debtors, to the extent that such proceeds are applied to payment of the obligation for the purpose of which the insurance was so issued.

Annuity Contract:

Any benefit, right, privilege and option in excess of $350 are subject to attachment after court evaluation. The $350 limitation does not apply in a bankruptcy proceeding however limited to contributions made within twelve months of bankruptcy filing in excess of 15% of the debtor's gross income.

Montana Code Annotated – Section 33-15-514-Exemption from execution of annuity contracts – Assignability of rights.

(1) The benefits, rights, privileges, and options which under any annuity contract heretofore or hereafter issued are due or prospectively due the annuitant shall not be subject to execution, nor shall the annuitant be compelled to exercise any such rights, powers, or options, nor shall creditors be allowed to interfere with or terminate the contract, except:

> as to amounts paid for or as premium on any such annuity with intent to defraud creditors, with interest thereon, and of which the creditor has given the insurer written notice at its home office prior to the making of the payments to the annuitant out of which the creditor seeks to recover. Any such notice shall specify the amount claimed or such facts as will enable the insurer to ascertain such amount and shall set forth such facts as will enable the insurer to ascertain the annuity contract, the annuitant, and the payments sought to be avoided on the ground of fraud.

> the total exemption of benefits presently due and payable to

any annuitant periodically or at stated times under all annuity contracts under which he is an annuitant shall not at any time exceed $250 per month for the length of time represented by such installments and that such periodic payments in excess of $350 per month shall be subject to garnishee execution; if the total benefits presently due and payable to any annuitant under all annuity contracts under which he is an annuitant shall at any time exceed payment at the rate of $350 per month, then the court may order such annuitant to pay to a judgment creditor or apply on the judgment, in installments, such portion of such excess benefits as to the court may appear just and proper, after due regard for the reasonable requirements of the judgment debtor and his family, if dependent upon him, as well as any payments required to be made by the annuitant to other creditors under prior court orders.

(2) If the contract so provides, the benefits, rights, privileges, or options accruing under such contract to a beneficiary or assignee shall not be transferable or subject to commutation, and if the benefits are payable periodically or at stated times, the same exemptions contained herein for the annuitant shall apply with respect to such beneficiary or assignee.

Montana Code Annotated – Section 31-2-106- Exempt property – Bankruptcy proceeding

An individual may not exempt from the property of the estate in any bankruptcy proceeding the property specified in 11 U.S.C. 522(d). An individual may exempt from the property of the estate in any bankruptcy proceeding:

(1) that property exempt from execution of judgment as provided in 19-2-1004, 19-18-612, 19-19-504, 19-20-706, 19-21-212, Title 25, chapter 13, part 6, 33-7-522, 33-15-512 through 33-15-514, 39-51-3105, 39-71-743, 39-73-110, 53-2-607, 53-9-129, Title 70, chapter 32, and 80-2-245;

(2) the individual's right to receive unemployment compensation and unemployment benefits; and

(3) the individual's right to receive benefits from or interest in a private or governmental retirement, pension, stock bonus, profit-sharing, annuity, or similar plan or contract on account of illness, disability, death, age, or length of service, excluding that portion of contributions made by the individual within 1 year before the filing of the petition in bankruptcy that exceeds 15% of the individual's gross income for that 1-year period, unless:

> the plan or contract was established by or under the auspices of an insider that employed the individual at the time the individual's rights under the plan or contract arose;
>
> the benefit is paid on account of age or length of service; and
>
> the plan or contract does not qualify under section 401(a), 403(a), 403(b), 408, or 409 of the Internal Revenue Code, 26 U.S.C. 401(a), 403(b), 408, or 409.

Nebraska

Life Insurance and Annuity Contract:

Proceeds, cash values and benefits under a life insurance policy or an annuity contract are exempt. The exemptions is limited to a total value of $100,000 for all matured and unmatured life insurance policies.

Nebraska Revised Statutes – Section 44-371 – Annuity contract; insurance proceeds and benefits; exempt from claims of creditors; exceptions.

(1) (a) Except as provided in subdivision (1)(b) of this section, all proceeds, cash values, and benefits accruing under any annuity contract, under any policy or certificate of life insurance payable upon the death of the insured to a beneficiary other than the estate of the insured, or under any accident or health insurance policy shall be exempt from attachment, garnishment, or other legal or equitable process and from all claims of creditors of the insured and of the beneficiary if related to the insured by

blood or marriage, unless a written assignment to the contrary has been obtained by the claimant.

(b) Subdivision (1)(a) of this section shall not apply to:

(i) An individual's aggregate interests greater than one hundred thousand dollars in all loan values or cash values of all matured or unmatured life insurance contracts and in all proceeds, cash values, or benefits accruing under all annuity contracts owned by such individual; and

(ii) An individual's interest in all loan values or cash values of all matured or unmatured life insurance contracts and in all proceeds, cash values, or benefits accruing under all annuity contracts owned by such individual, to the extent that the loan values or cash values of any matured or unmatured life insurance contract or the proceeds, cash values, or benefits accruing under any annuity contract were established or increased through contributions, premiums, or any other payments made within three years prior to bankruptcy or within three years prior to entry against the individual of a money judgment which thereafter becomes final.

(c) An insurance company shall not be liable or responsible to any person to determine or ascertain the existence or identity of any such creditors prior to payment of any such loan values, cash values, proceeds, or benefits.

(2) Notwithstanding subsection (1) of this section, proceeds, cash values, and benefits accruing under any annuity contract or under any policy or certificate of life insurance payable upon the death of the insured to a beneficiary other than the estate of the insured shall not be exempt from attachment, garnishment, or other legal or equitable process by a judgment creditor of the beneficiary if the judgment against the beneficiary was based on, arose from, or was related to an act, transaction, or course of conduct for which the beneficiary has been convicted by any court of a crime punishable only by life imprisonment or death. No insurance company shall be liable or responsible to any person to determine or ascertain the existence or identity of any such judgment creditor prior to payment of any such proceeds, cash values, or benefits. This

subsection shall apply to any judgment rendered on or after January 1, 1995, irrespective of when the criminal conviction is or was rendered and irrespective of whether proceedings for attachment, garnishment, or other legal or equitable process were pending on March 14, 1997.

Nevada

Life Insurance:

Life insurance policies, proceeds and avails are exempt.

Nevada Revised Statutes – Section 687B.260 – Exemption of proceeds of certain policies.

1. If a policy of insurance, whether issued before, on or after January 1, 1972, is effected by any person on his or her own life, or on another life, in favor of a person other than himself or herself, or, except in cases of transfer with intent to defraud creditors, if a policy of life insurance is assigned or in any way made payable to any such person, the lawful beneficiary or assignee thereof, other than the insured or the person so effecting such insurance or executors or administrators of the insured or the person so effecting such insurance, is entitled to its proceeds and avails against the creditors and representatives of the insured and of the person effecting the same, whether or not the right to change the beneficiary is reserved or permitted and whether or not the policy is made payable to the person whose life is insured or to the executors or administrators of such person if the beneficiary or assignee predeceases the person. Except as otherwise provided in this subsection, such proceeds and avails are exempt from all liability for any debt of the beneficiary existing at the time the proceeds and avails are made available for the use of the beneficiary. Subject to the statute of limitations, the amount of any premiums for such insurance paid with intent to defraud creditors, with interest thereon, inures to the benefit of the creditors from the proceeds of the policy. The insurer issuing the policy is discharged of all liability thereon by payment of its

proceeds in accordance with its terms, unless, before the payment, the insurer has received written notice at its home office, by or in behalf of a creditor, of a claim to recover for transfer made or premiums paid with intent to defraud creditors, with specification of the amount claimed along with such facts as will assist the insurer to ascertain the particular policy.

2. For the purposes of subsection 1, a policy shall also be deemed to be payable to a person other than the insured if and to the extent that a facility-of-payment clause or a similar clause in the policy permits the insurer to discharge its obligation after the death of the individual insured by paying the death benefits to a person as permitted by such a clause.

3. This section does not apply to insurance issued pursuant to this Code to a creditor covering his or her debtors to the extent that such proceeds are applied to payment of the obligation for the purpose of which the insurance was so issued.

Nevada Revised Statutes – Section 21.090(k) – Property exempt from execution.

(k) All money, benefits, privileges or immunities accruing or in any manner growing out of any life insurance.

Annuity Contract:

The benefits, rights, privileges and options under an annuity contract are exempt.

Nevada Revised Statutes – Section 687B.290 – Exemption of proceeds: Annuities; assignability of rights.

1. The benefits, rights, privileges and options which under any annuity contract issued prior to or after January 1, 1972, are due or prospectively due the annuitant shall not be subject to execution nor shall the annuitant be compelled to exercise any such rights, powers or options, nor shall creditors be allowed to interfere with or terminate the contract, except as to amounts paid for or as premium on any such annuity with intent to defraud creditors, with interest thereon, and of which the creditor has given the insurer written

notice at its home office prior to the making of the payment to the annuitant out of which the creditor seeks to recover. Any such notice shall specify the amount claimed or such facts as will enable the insurer to ascertain such amount, and shall set forth such facts as will enable the insurer to ascertain the annuity contract, the annuitant and the payment sought to be avoided on the ground of fraud.

2. If the contract so provides, the benefits, rights, privileges or options accruing under such contract to a beneficiary or assignee shall not be transferable or subject to commutation, and the same exemptions and exceptions contained in this section for the annuitant shall apply with respect to such beneficiary or assignee.

New Hampshire

Life Insurance:

Policies of life insurance created to benefit of a married woman or for the benefit of another person are exempt.

New Hampshire Revised Statutes Annotated – Section 408:1 – Married Women.

Every policy of life or endowment insurance made payable to or for the benefit of a married woman, or after its issue assigned, transferred, or in any way made payable to a married woman or to any person in trust for her or her benefit, whether procured by herself, her husband, or by any other person and whether the assignment or transfer is made by her husband or by any other person, shall enure to her separate use and benefit, and to that of her children, subject to the provisions of law, relative to premiums paid in fraud of creditors.

New Hampshire Revised Statutes Annotated – Section 408:2 – Third Person.

Every policy of life or endowment insurance made payable to or for the benefit of a married woman, or after its issue assigned, transferred, or in any way made payable to a married woman or to any person in trust for her or her benefit, whether procured by herself, her husband, or by any other person and whether the assignment or transfer is made by her husband or by any other person, shall enure to her separate use and benefit, and to that of her children, subject to the provisions of law, relative to premiums paid in fraud of creditors.

Annuity Contract:

Annuity contracts are exempt if structured as a retirement plan.

New Hampshire Revised Statutes Annotated – Section 511:2 – Exemptions

XIX. Subject to the Uniform Fraudulent Transfer Act, RSA 545-A, any interest in a retirement plan or arrangement qualified for tax exemption purposes under present or future acts of Congress; provided, any transfer or rollover contribution between retirement plans shall not be deemed a transfer which is fraudulent as to a creditor under the Uniform Fraudulent Transfer Act. "Retirement plan or arrangement qualified for tax exemption purposes" shall include without limitation, trusts, custodial accounts, insurance, annuity contracts, and other properties and rights constituting a part thereof. By way of example and not by limitation, retirement plans or arrangements qualified for tax exemption purposes permitted under present acts of Congress include defined contribution plans and defined benefit plans as defined under the Internal Revenue Code (IRC), individual retirement accounts including Roth IRAs and education IRAs, individual retirement annuities, simplified employee pension plans, Keogh plans, IRC section 403(a) annuity plans, IRC section 403(b) annuities, and eligible state deferred compensation plans governed under IRC section 457. This paragraph shall be in addition to and not a limitation of any other provision of New Hampshire law which grants an exemption from attachment or execution and every other species of forced sale for the payment of debts. This paragraph shall be effective for retirement plans and arrangements in existence on, or created after

January 1, 1999, but shall apply only to extensions of credit made, and debts arising, after January 1, 1999.

New Jersey

Life Insurance:

Life insurance proceeds are exempt if affected for someone other than the insured.

New Jersey Statutes Annotated – Section 17B:24-6 – Exemption of proceeds – life insurance.

a. If a policy of insurance, whether heretofore or hereafter issued, is affected by any person on his own life, or on another life, in favor of a person other than himself, or, except in cases of transfer with intent to defraud creditors, if a policy of life insurance is assigned or in any way made payable to any such person, then the lawful beneficiary, assignee or payee of such policy, shall be entitled to its proceeds and avails against the creditors and representatives of the insured and of the person effecting the same, whether or not the right to change the beneficiary is reserved or permitted, or the policy is made payable to the person whose life is insured or to the executors or administrators of such person if the beneficiary shall predecease such person.

Except however the foregoing shall not be applicable if the lawful beneficiary, assignee or payee of such policy is any of the following:

(1) The insured,

(2) The person so effecting such insurance, or

(3) The executors or administrators of such insured or the person so effecting such insurance.

b. Such proceeds and avails shall be exempt from any liability for any debt of the beneficiary existing at the time the proceeds and avails become available for his use; provided that, subject to the statute of limitations, the amount of any premiums for such insurance paid with intent to defraud creditors, with interest thereon, shall inure to their benefit from the proceeds of the policy; but the insurer issuing the policy shall be discharged of all liability thereon by payment of its proceeds in accordance with its terms, unless, before such payment, the insurer shall have received written notice at its home office, by or in behalf of a creditor, of a claim to recover for transfer made or premiums paid with intent to defraud creditors setting forth such facts as will enable the insurer to ascertain the particular policy.

c. For the purposes of subsections a. and b. above, a policy shall also be deemed to be payable to a person other than the insured if and to the extent that a facility-of-payment clause or similar clause in the policy permits the insurer to discharge its obligation after the death of the individual insured by paying the death benefits to a person as permitted by such clause.

Annuity Contract:

Annuity contract benefits are exempt up to $500 per month.

New Jersey Statutes Annotated – Section 17B:24-7 – Exemption of proceeds – annuity contracts.

a. The benefits, rights, privileges, powers and options which under any annuity contract heretofore or hereafter issued are due or prospectively due the annuitant, shall not be subject to execution, garnishment, attachment, sequestration or other legal process nor shall the annuitant be compelled to exercise any such rights, privileges, powers, or options, nor shall creditors be allowed to interfere with or terminate the contract, except:

(1) As to amounts paid, with intent to defraud creditors, for or as consideration for any such annuity, with interest thereon, and of which the creditor has given the insurer written notice at its home office prior to the making of the payments to the annuitant out of which the creditor seeks to recover. Any such notice shall set forth such facts as will enable the insurer to ascertain the particular annuity contract.

(2) The total exemption of benefits presently due and payable to any annuitant periodically or at stated times under all annuity contracts under which he is an annuitant, shall not at any time exceed $500.00 per month for the length of time represented by such installments, and such periodic payments in excess of $500.00 per month shall be subject to garnishee execution to the same extent as are wages and salaries.

(3) If the total benefits presently due and payable to any annuitant under all annuity contracts under which he is an annuitant, shall at any time exceed payment at the rate of $500.00 per month, then the court may order such annuitant to pay to a judgment creditor or apply on the judgment, in installments, such portion of such excess benefits as to the court may appear just and proper, after due regard for the reasonable requirements of the judgment debtor and his family, if dependent upon him as well as any prior court orders.

b. If the contract so provides, the benefits, rights, privileges, powers or options accruing under such contract to a beneficiary or assignee shall not be transferable nor subject to commutation, and if the benefits are payable periodically or at stated times, the same exemptions and exceptions contained herein for the annuitant, shall apply with respect to such beneficiary or assignee.

New Mexico

Life Insurance and Annuity Contracts:

Life insurance and annuity contract cash surrender value is exempt.

Proceeds of a life insurance policy are exempt

New Mexico Statutes Annotated – Section 42-10-3 – Life, accident and health insurance benefits.

The cash surrender value of any life insurance policy, the withdrawal value of any optional settlement, annuity contract or deposit with any life insurance company, all weekly, monthly, quarterly, semiannual or annual annuities, indemnities or payments of every kind from any life, accident or health insurance policy, annuity contract or deposit heretofore or hereafter issued upon the life of a citizen or resident of the state of New Mexico, or made by any such insurance company with such citizen, upon whatever form and whether the insured or the person protected thereby has the right to change the beneficiary therein or not, shall in no case be liable to attachment, garnishment or legal process in favor of any creditor of the person whose life is so insured or who is protected by said contract, or who receives or is to receive the benefit thereof, nor shall it be subject in any other manner to the debts of the person whose life is so insured, or who is protected by said contract or who receives or is to receive the benefit thereof, unless such policy, contract or deposit be taken out, made or assigned in writing for the benefit of such creditor.

New Mexico Statutes Annotated – Section 42-10-5 – Life insurance proceeds.

The proceeds of any life insurance are not subject to the debts of the deceased, except by special contract or arrangement, to be made in writing.

New York

Life Insurance:

A beneficiary's interest in the proceeds and avails of a life insurance policy are exempt provided the beneficiary is not the owner or insured.

If the owner is a spouse of the insured the proceeds and avails of a life insurance policy are exempt.

Accelerated benefits paid to the owner of a life insurance policy are exempt.

New York Insurance Law – Section 3212(b) – Exemption of proceeds and avails of certain insurance and annuity contracts.

(b) (1) If a policy of insurance has been or shall be effected by any person on his own life in favor of a third person beneficiary, or made payable otherwise to a third person, such third person shall be entitled to the proceeds and avails of such policy as against the creditors, personal representatives, trustees in bankruptcy and receivers in state and federal courts of the person effecting the insurance.

(2) If a policy of insurance has been or shall be effected upon the life of another person in favor of the person effecting the same or made payable otherwise to such person, the latter shall be entitled to the proceeds and avails of such policy as against the creditors, personal representatives, trustees in bankruptcy and receivers in state and federal courts of the person insured. If the person effecting such insurance shall be the spouse of the insured, he or she shall be entitled to the proceeds and avails of such policy as against his or her own creditors, trustees in bankruptcy and receivers in state and federal courts.

(3) If a policy of insurance has been or shall be effected by any person on the life of another person in favor of a third person beneficiary, or made payable otherwise to a third person, such third person shall be entitled to the proceeds and avails of such policy as against the creditors, personal representatives, trustees in bankruptcy and receivers in state and federal courts of the person insured and of the person effecting the insurance.

(4) (A) The person insured pursuant to paragraph one of this subsection or the person effecting the insurance other than the spouse of the insured pursuant to paragraph two hereof, and the person effecting the insurance pursuant to paragraph three hereof, or the executor or administrator of any such persons, or a person entitled to the proceeds or avails of such policy in trust for such persons shall not be deemed a third person beneficiary, assignee or payee. (B) A policy shall be deemed payable to a third person beneficiary if and to the extent that a facility-of-payment clause

or similar clause in the policy permits the insurer to discharge its obligation after the death of the person insured by paying the death benefits to a third person.

(5) This section shall be applicable whether or not the right is reserved in any such policy to change the designated beneficiary and whether or not the policy is made payable to the person whose life is insured if the beneficiary, assignee or payee shall predecease such person; and no person shall be compelled to exercise any rights, powers, options or privileges under such policy.

(6) If a policy of insurance has been or shall be effected by any person on his own life or upon the life of another person, the policyowner shall be entitled to any accelerated payments of the death benefit or accelerated payment of a special surrender value permitted under such policy as against the creditors, personal representatives, trustees in bankruptcy and receivers in state and federal courts of the policyowner.

Annuity Contract:

Provided there is not an intent to hinder, delay, or defraud creditors the proceeds of an annuity contract are exempt.

New York Insurance Law – Section 3212(b) – Exemption of proceeds and avails of certain insurance and annuity contracts.

(d) (1) The benefits, rights, privileges and options which, under any annuity contract are due or prospectively due the annuitant, who paid the consideration for the annuity contract, shall not be subject to execution.

(2) The annuitant shall not be compelled to exercise any such rights, powers or options contained in the annuity contract, nor shall creditors be allowed to interfere with or terminate the contract, except as provided in subsection (e) hereof and except that the court may order the annuitant to pay to a judgment creditor or apply on the judgment in installments, a portion of such benefits that appears just and proper to the court, with due regard for the reasonable requirements of the

judgment debtor and his family, if dependent upon him, as well as any payments required to be made by the annuitant to other creditors under prior court orders.

(3) The benefits, rights, privileges or options accruing under such contract to a beneficiary or assignee shall not be transferable nor subject to commutation. If the benefits are payable periodically or at stated times, the same exemptions and exceptions contained herein for the annuitant shall apply with respect to such beneficiary or assignee.

(4) The benefits, rights, privileges or options accruing under an annuity contract funding a structured settlement which would otherwise be nontransferable under this subsection may be transferred in accordance with title seventeen of article five of the general obligations law. As used in this paragraph the term "structured settlement" means an arrangement for periodic payments of damages for personal injuries established by settlement or judgment in resolution of a tort claim; and the term "periodic payments" shall include scheduled future lump sum payments.

North Carolina

Life Insurance:
Beneficiary's interest in the proceeds or a life insurance policy are exempt, provided the beneficiary is not the insured.

North Carolina General Statutes – 58-58-115 – Creditors deprived of benefits of life insurance policies except in cases of fraud.

If a policy of insurance is effected by any person on his own life or on another life in favor of a person other than himself, or, except in cases of transfer with intent to defraud creditors, if a policy of life insurance is assigned or in any way made payable to any such person, the lawful beneficiary or assignee thereof, other than the insured or the person so effecting such insurance or the executor or administrator of such insured or of the person effecting such insurance, shall be entitled to its proceeds and avails against creditors and representatives of the insured and of the person effecting same, whether or not the right to change the beneficiary is reserved or permitted, and whether or not the policy is made payable to the person whose life is insured if the beneficiary or assignee shall predecease such person: Provided, that subject to the statute of limitations, the amount of any premiums for said insurance paid with the intent to defraud creditors, with interest thereon, shall inure to their benefit from the proceeds of the policy; but the company issuing the policy shall be discharged of all liability thereon by payment of its proceeds in accordance with its terms unless, before such payment, the company shall have written notice by or in behalf of the creditor, of a claim to recover for transfer made or premiums paid with intent to defraud creditors, with specifications of the amount claimed.

Annuity Contract: No specific statute.

North Dakota

Life Insurance:

Life insurance surrender value is exempt if payable to the spouse, child or dependent of the insured.

The proceeds of a life insurance policy are exempt when payable to the deceased, a personal representative, heirs or estate of the deceased.

North Dakota Century Code – Section 26.1-33-36 – Rights in life policies exempt from claims of creditors.

The surrender value of any life insurance policy which, upon the death of the insured, would be payable to the spouse, children, or any relative of the insured dependent, or likely to be dependent, upon the insured for support, is exempt absolutely from the claims of creditors of the insured to the extent provided in section 28-22-

03.1. No creditor of the insured, and no court or officer of a court acting for any such creditors, may elect for the insured to have the life insurance policy surrendered or in anywise converted into money, and no life insurance policy or property right in the policy belonging to the holder, except for the value thereof in excess of the amount provided by section 28-22-03.1, may be subject to seizure under any process of any court under any circumstance.

North Dakota Century Code – Section 26.1-33-40 – Avails of life policy payable to deceased or to the deceased's heirs, personal representatives, or estate – Exemption – Distribution.

The avails of a life insurance policy or of a contract payable by any mutual aid or benevolent society, when made payable to the deceased, to the personal representatives of the deceased, to the deceased's heirs, or to the deceased's estate, is not subject to the debts of the decedent upon the death of the insured or member of the society except by special contract. The avails must be inventoried as a part of the estate of the decedent and must be considered as part of the general assets of the estate. The insured may transfer the avails of the life insurance policy or contract either by will or by contract. Nothing contained in this section affects, in any manner, any life insurance policy or beneficiary certificate which is made payable to a designated person, including the spouse of the insured, or to persons or to members of a family designated as a class, such as "all children" or "all brothers and sisters", even though the members of the class are not designated by name; or permits any insured to dispose of the avails of a contract by a mutual or fraternal society by will to anyone who could not be a beneficiary in the contract under the charter or bylaws of the society.

Annuity Contract:

Annuity contract is exempt if qualified under Section 401(a), 4039a), 4039b) or 408 of the Internal Revenue Code.

North Dakota Century Code – Section 28-22-03.1 – Additional exemptions for residents.

e. A payment under a stock bonus, pension, profit-sharing, annuity, or similar plan or contract on account of illness, disability, death, age, or length of service, to the extent reasonably necessary for the support of the debtor and any dependent of the debtor, unless:

(1) That plan or contract was established by or under the auspices of an insider that employed the debtor at the time the debtor's rights under that plan or contract arose;

(2) That payment is on account of age or length of service; and

(3) That plan or contract does not qualify under section 401(a), 403(a), 403(b), or 408 of the Internal Revenue Code of 1986.

Ohio

Life Insurance and Annuity Contract:

The proceeds and avails of an insurance policy and annuity contract are exempt if the beneficiary is the owner's spouse, children or other dependents.

Ohio Revised Code Annotated – Section 3911.10 – Exemption of proceeds from claims of creditors.

All contracts of life or endowment insurance or annuities upon the life of any person, or any interest therein, which may hereafter mature and which have been taken out for the benefit of, or made payable by change of beneficiary, transfer, or assignment to, the spouse or children, or any persons dependent upon such person, or an institution or entity described in division (B)(1) of section 3911.09 of the Revised Code, or any creditor, or to a trustee for the benefit of such spouse, children, dependent persons, institution or entity, or creditor, shall be held, together with the proceeds or avails of such contracts, subject to a change of beneficiary if desired, free from all claims of the creditors of such insured person or annuitant. Subject to the statute of limitations, the amount of any premium upon such contracts, endowments, or annuities, paid in fraud of creditors, with interest thereon, shall inure to their benefit from the proceeds of the contracts, but the company issuing any such contract is discharged of all liability thereon by the payment of its proceeds in accordance with its terms, unless, before such payment, written notice is given to it by a creditor, specifying the amount of the claim and the premiums which the creditor alleges have been fraudulently paid.

Oklahoma

Life Insurance and Annuity Contract:

The proceeds and cash values under any insurance policy or annuity contract are exempt.

Oklahoma Statute Title 36 – Section 3631.1(A) – Benefits Rendered to Insured or Beneficiary – Exemptions

All money or benefits of any kind, including policy proceeds and cash values, to be paid or rendered to the insured or any beneficiary under any policy of insurance issued by a life, health or accident insurance company, under any policy issued by a mutual benefit association, or under any plan or program of annuities and benefits, shall:

1. Inure exclusively to the benefit of the person for whose use and benefit the money or benefits are designated in the policy, plan or program;

2. Be fully exempt from execution, attachment, garnishment or other process;

3. Be fully exempt from being seized, taken or appropriated or applied by any legal or equitable process or operation of law to pay any debt or liability of the insured or of any beneficiary, either before or after said money or benefits is or are paid or rendered; and

4. Be fully exempt from all demands in any bankruptcy proceeding of the insured or beneficiary.

Oregon

Life Insurance:

The proceeds from a life insurance policy are exempt if for the benefit of someone other than the insured.

Group life insurance policies and the proceeds are exempt.

Oregon Revised Statutes – Section 743.046 – Exemption of proceeds of individual life insurance other than annuities.

(1) When a policy of insurance is effected by any person on any person's own life or on another life in favor of some person other than that person having an insurable interest in the life insured, the lawful beneficiary thereof, other than that person or that person's legal representative, is entitled to its proceeds against the creditors or representatives of the person effecting the policy.

(2) The person to whom a policy of life insurance is made payable may maintain an action thereon in the person's own name.

(3) A policy of life insurance payable to a beneficiary other than the estate of the insured, having by its terms a cash surrender value available to the insured, is exempt from execution issued from any court in this state and in the event of bankruptcy of such insured is exempt from all demands in legal proceeding under such bankruptcy.

(4) Subject to the statute of limitations, the amount of any premiums paid in fraud of creditors for such insurance, with interest thereon, shall inure to their benefit from the proceeds of the policy. The insurer issuing the policy shall be discharged of all liability thereon by payment of its proceeds in accordance with its terms unless, before such payment, the insurer has received at its home office written notice by or in behalf of some creditor, with specifications of the amount claimed, claiming to recover for certain premiums paid in fraud of creditors.

(5) The insured under any policy within this section shall not

be denied the right to change the beneficiary when such right is expressly reserved in the policy.

(6) This section does not apply to annuity policies.

Oregon Revised Statutes – Section 743.047 – Exemption of proceeds of group life insurance.

(1) A policy of group life insurance or the proceeds thereof payable to a person or persons other than the individual insured or the individual's estate shall be exempt from debts and claims of creditors or representatives of the individual insured and, in the event of bankruptcy of the individual insured, from all demands in legal proceedings under such bankruptcy.

(2) The provisions of subsection (1) of this section do not apply to group life insurance issued to a creditor covering the creditor's debtors to the extent that such proceeds are applied to payment of the obligation for the purpose of which the insurance was so issued.

Annuity Contract:

Up to $500 per month is exempted in the benefits, rights, privileges, and options under an annuity contract.

Oregon Revised Statutes – Section 743.047 – Exemption of proceeds of annuity policies; assignability of rights.

(1) The benefits, rights, privileges and options which are due or prospectively due an annuitant under any annuity policy issued before, on or after June 8, 1967, shall not be subject to execution, nor shall the annuitant be compelled to exercise any such rights, powers or options, nor shall creditors be allowed to interfere with or terminate the policy, except:

(a) As to amounts paid for or as premium on any such annuity with intent to defraud creditors, with interest thereon, and of which the creditor has given the insurer written notice at its home office prior to the making of the payments to the annuitant out of which the creditor seeks to recover. Any such notice shall specify the amount claimed or such facts as will enable the insurer to ascertain such amount, and shall set forth such facts as will enable the insurer to ascertain the annuity policy, the annuitant and the payments sought to be avoided on the ground of fraud.

(b) The total exemption of benefits presently due and payable to any annuitant periodically or at stated times under all annuity policies under which the person is an annuitant shall not at any time exceed $500 per month for the length of time represented by such installments. Such periodic payments in excess of $500 per month shall be subject to garnishee execution to the same extent as are wages and salaries.

(c) If the total benefits presently due and payable to any annuitant under all annuity policies under which the person is an annuitant shall at any time exceed payment at the rate of $500 per month, the court may order such annuitant to pay to a judgment creditor or apply on the judgment, in installments, the portion of such excess benefits as to the court may appear just and proper, after due regard for the reasonable requirements of the judgment debtor and family, if dependent upon the judgment debtor, as well as any payments required to be made by the annuitant to other creditors under prior court orders.

(2) If the policy so provides, the benefits, rights, privileges or options accruing under the policy to a beneficiary or assignee shall not be transferable nor subject to commutation, and if the benefits are payable periodically or at stated times, the same exemptions and exceptions contained in this section for the annuitant shall apply with respect to such beneficiary or assignee.

Pennsylvania

Life Insurance:

Life insurance proceeds are exempt if the policy or supplemental agreement provides that the proceeds and income is not assignable.

If the policy is created to benefit a spouse, child or dependent of the insured the proceeds are exempt unless the spouse, child or dependent is the judgment creditor.

Group life insurance policies are exempt.

42 Pennsylvania Constitution Statutes – Section 8124(c) (4); (5); and (6) – Exemption of Insurance Proceeds

(c) The following property or other rights of the judgment debtor shall be exempt from attachment or execution on a judgment:

(4) Any amount of proceeds retained by the insurer at maturity or otherwise under the terms of an annuity or policy of life insurance if the policy or a supplemental agreement provides that such proceeds and the income therefrom shall not be assignable.

(5) Any policy of group insurance or the proceeds thereof.

(6) The net amount payable under any annuity contract or policy of life insurance made for the benefit of or assigned to the spouse, children or dependent relative of the insured, whether or not the right to change the named beneficiary is reserved by or permitted to the insured. The preceding sentence shall not be applicable to the extent the judgment debtor is such spouse, child or other relative.

Annuity:

Annuity are exempt up to $100 per month.

42 Pennsylvania Constitution Statutes – Section 8124(c) (3) – Exemption of Insurance Proceeds

(3) Any policy or contract of insurance or annuity issued to a solvent insured who is the beneficiary thereof, except any part thereof exceeding an income or return of $100 per month.

Rhode Island

Life Insurance and Annuity Contract:

Life insurance and annuity contract proceeds are exempt if stated in the policy.

Rhode Island General Laws – Section 27-4-12 – Provision for exemption from encumbrance, transfer, or claims of creditors.

Any policy of life or endowment insurance or any annuity contract may provide that the proceeds of or payments under it shall not be subject to transfer, anticipation, or commutation or encumbrance by any beneficiary other than the insured or the purchaser of the annuity, and shall not be subject to the claims of a creditor of any beneficiary or any legal process against the beneficiary.

South Carolina

Life Insurance:

Proceeds and cash value of life insurance are exempt if used for support of spouse, children and dependents of the insured.

Unmatured life insurance is exempt up to $4,000 on any accrued dividend, interest or loan value.

Group life insurance proceeds are exempt.

South Carolina Code Annotated – Section 38-63-40(A) and (C) – Life insurance proceeds for insured's spouse, children, or dependents exempt from claims of insured's creditors; exceptions; certain other proceeds exempt from claims of beneficiary's or insured's creditors.

(A) Proceeds and cash surrender values of life insurance payable to a beneficiary other than the insured's estate in which such proceeds and cash surrender values are expressed to be for the primary benefit of the insured's spouse, children, or dependents are exempt from creditors of the insured whether or not the right to change the beneficiary is reserved and whether or not the policy is payable to the insured if the beneficiary dies first except:

(1) if the insured has filed a petition in bankruptcy within two years of purchasing the insurance, such proceeds or cash surrender are only exempt as permitted by Section 15-41-30; or

(2) the amount of premiums paid and interest thereon with intent to defraud creditors;

(3) a creditor possessing a valid assignment from the policy owner may recover from either the cash surrender value or the proceeds of the life insurance policy the amount secured by the assignment with interest.

(C) Proceeds of group life insurance contracts are exempt from claims of the creditors of the insured.

Annuity Contract:

Annuity contract proceeds are exempt.

South Carolina Code Annotated – Section 38-63-40(B)

(B) Proceeds of life insurance or annuity contracts, by agreement, may be held by the insurer exempt from claims of the beneficiary's creditors.

South Dakota

Life Insurance:

Up to $20,000 of proceeds of life and health insurance are exempt.

South Dakota Codified Laws – Section 58-12-4 – Life and health insurance – Exemption of benefits and proceeds from execution.

The proceeds of a policy of life or health insurance to the total amount of twenty thousand dollars only, in the absence of any agreement or assignment to the contrary, shall inure to the separate use of the insured, his surviving spouse, or children, as the case may be, independently of the creditors of any of them and shall not be subject to the payment of the debts of any one or all of such persons, notwithstanding that the proceeds may be payable directly to the insured or surviving spouse or children as the named beneficiary or beneficiaries or otherwise; and the proceeds of an endowment policy, payable to the insured on attaining a certain age, to the extent of twenty thousand dollars shall at all times be exempted from the debts of such spouse or children of the insured; and the avails of any life or health insurance or other sum of money not exceeding twenty thousand dollars made payable by any mutual aid or benevolent society to any member or beneficiary spouse or children or both shall likewise be exempt.

Annuity Contract:

Up to $250 of proceeds of benefits, rights, privileges and options are exempt.

South Dakota Codified Laws – Section 58-12-6 – Exemption of annuity contract benefits, rights, privileges, and options from execution.

The benefits, rights, privileges, and options which under any annuity contract heretofore or hereafter issued are due or prospectively due the annuitant, shall not be subject to execution nor shall the annuitant be compelled to exercise any such rights, powers, or options, nor shall creditors be allowed to interfere with or terminate the contract, except as provided by §§ 58-12-7 to 58-12-9, inclusive.

South Dakota Codified Laws – Section 58-12-8 – Maximum amount of annuity exemption – Excess subject to levy.

The total exemption under § 58-12-6 of benefits presently due and payable to any annuitant periodically or at stated times under all annuity contracts under which he is an annuitant, shall not at any time exceed two hundred and fifty dollars per month for the length of time represented by such installments, and such periodic payments in excess of two hundred and fifty dollars per month shall be subject to levy in the manner provided by law and the rules of court.

Tennessee

Life Insurance and Annuity Contract:

Life insurance benefits payable to a surviving spouse, children and dependents are exempt.

The net amount payable under a policy of a life insurance policy or an annuity contract affected for the benefit of the annuitant's spouse, children or dependent's are exempt.

Tennessee Code Annotated – Section 56-7-201 – Life insurance payable to surviving spouse and children – Effect of Proceeds being payable to estate.

On the death of an insured, any life insurance acquired by the insured or the insured's spouse and payable to the intestate insured's estate benefits the surviving spouse and children and the proceeds shall be divided between them according to the statutes of distribution without being in any manner subject to the debts of the decedent. If the proceeds of the insurance are payable to the estate of a testate decedent or the trustee of a revocable trust of which the decedent was a settlor, the proceeds shall pass as part of the estate or trust and under the dispositive provisions of the will or trust agreement, as ordinary cash, whether or not the will or trust agreement uses any apt or express words referring to the insurance proceeds, but the proceeds shall not be subject to the debts of the decedent unless specifically charged with the debts in the will or trust agreement.

Tennessee Code Annotated – Section 56-7-203 – Life insurance or annuity for or assigned to spouse or children or dependent relatives exempt from claims of creditors.

The net amount payable under any policy of life insurance or under any annuity contract upon the life of any person made for the benefit of, or assigned to, the spouse and/or children, or dependent relatives of the persons, shall be exempt from all claims of the creditors of the person arising out of or based upon any obligation created after January 1, 1932, whether or not the right to change the named beneficiary is reserved by or permitted to that person.

Texas

Life Insurance and Annuity Contract:

Life insurance proceeds and cash value are exempt. Annuity contracts are exempt.

Texas Insurance Code – Section 1108.51 – Exemptions for certain insurance and annuity benefits.

(a) Except as provided by Section 1108.053, this section applies to any benefits, including the cash value and proceeds of an insurance policy, to be provided to an insured or beneficiary under:

an insurance policy or annuity contract issued by a life, health, or accident insurance company, including a mutual company or fraternal benefit society; or

an annuity or benefit plan used by an employer or individual.

(b) Notwithstanding any other provision of this code, insurance or annuity benefits described by Subsection (a):

inure exclusively to the benefit of the person for whose use and benefit the insurance or annuity is designated in the policy or contract; and are fully exempt from:

> (A) garnishment, attachment, execution, or other seizure;

> (B) seizure, appropriation, or application by any legal or equitable process or by operation of law to pay a debt or other liability of an insured or of a beneficiary, either before or after the benefits are provided; and

> (C) a demand in a bankruptcy proceeding of the insured or beneficiary.

Texas Insurance Code – Section 1108.53 – Exceptions to exemptions.

The exemptions provided by Section 1108.051 do not apply to:

> (1) a premium payment made in fraud of a creditor, subject to the applicable statute of limitations for recovering the payment;

> (2) a debt of the insured or beneficiary secured by a pledge of the insurance policy or the proceeds of the policy; or

> (3) a child support lien or levy under Chapter 157, Family Code.

Utah

Life Insurance:

Life insurance proceeds, benefits and avails are exempt.

Utah Code Annotated – Section 78-23-5(1)(a)(B)(xi) and (xii) – Property exempt from execution.

> (a) An individual is entitled to exemption of the following property:

> (B) produced by the debtor or the debtor and his resident family;

>> (xi) proceeds or benefits of life insurance contracts payable on the death of the insured, if the individual

was the spouse or a dependent of the insured;

(xii) proceeds and avails of any unmatured life insurance contract owned by the individual;

Annuity Contract:

Annuity contracts are exempt if payable to the individual as a beneficiary.

Utah Code Annotated – Section 78-23-5(1)(a)(B)(xiii)(B) – Property exempt from execution.

(a) An individual is entitled to exemption of the following property:

(B) produced by the debtor or the debtor and his resident family;

(xiii) except as provided in Subsection (1)(b), any money or other assets held for or

payable to the individual as a participant or beneficiary from or an interest of the individual as a participant or beneficiary in:

(B) an annuity as defined in Section 31A-1-301; and

Vermont

Life Insurance:

Life insurance proceeds are exempt.

Group life and disability insurance proceeds are exempt.

Vermont Statutes Annotated – Title 8 – Section 3706 – Exemption of proceeds – Life Insurance

(a) If a policy of insurance, whether heretofore or hereafter issued, is effected by any person on his or her own life, or on another life, in favor of a person other than himself or herself, or, except in cases of transfer with intent to defraud creditors, if a policy of life insurance is assigned or in any way made payable to any such person, the lawful beneficiary or assignee thereof, other than the insured or the person so effecting such insurance or executors or administrators of such insured or the person so effecting such insurance, shall be entitled to its proceeds and avails against the creditors and representatives of the insured and of the person effecting the same, whether or not the right to change the beneficiary is reserved or permitted, and whether or not the policy is made payable to the person whose life is insured if the beneficiary or assignee shall predecease such person, and such proceeds and avails shall be exempt from all liability for any debt of the beneficiary existing at the time the policy is made available for his or her use: Provided, that subject to the statute of limitations, the amount of any premiums for such insurance paid with intent to defraud creditors, with interest thereon, shall inure to their benefit from the proceeds of the policy; but the insurer issuing the policy shall be discharged of all liability thereon by payment of its proceeds in accordance with its terms, unless, before such payment, the insurer shall have received written notice at its home office, by or in behalf of a creditor, of a claim to recover for transfer made or premiums paid with intent to defraud creditors, with specification of the amount claimed along with such facts as will assist the insurer to identify the particular policy.

(b) For the purposes of subsection (a) of this section, a policy shall also be deemed to be payable to a person other than the insured if and to the extent that a facility-of-payment clause or similar clause in the policy permits the insurer to discharge its obligation after the death of the individual insured by paying the death benefits to a person as permitted by such clause.

Vermont Statutes Annotated – Title 8 – Section 3708 – Group insurance

(a) A policy of group life insurance or group disability insurance or the proceeds thereof payable to the individual insured or to the beneficiary thereunder, shall not be liable, either before or after payment, to be applied by any process to pay any debt or liability of such insured individual or his or her beneficiary or of any other person having a right under the policy. The proceeds thereof, when not made payable to a named beneficiary or to a third person pursuant to a facility-of-payment clause, shall not constitute a part of the estate of the individual insured for the payment of his or her debts.

(b) This section shall not apply to group insurance issued to a creditor covering his or her debtors, to the extent that such proceeds are applied to payment of the obligation for the purpose of which the insurance was so issued.

Annuity Contract:

Benefits up to $350 per month are exempt.

Vermont Statutes Annotated – Title 8 – Section 3709 – Annuity contracts – Assignability of rights

(a) The benefits, rights, privileges and options which under any annuity contract heretofore or hereafter issued are due or prospectively due the annuitant, shall not be subject to execution nor shall the annuitant be compelled to exercise any such rights, powers, or options, nor shall creditors be allowed to interfere with or terminate the contract, except:

(1) As to considerations paid for any such annuity with intent to defraud creditors, with interest thereon, and of which the creditor has given the insurer written notice at its home office prior to the making of the payments to the annuitant out of which the creditor seeks to recover. Any such notice shall specify the amount claimed or such facts as will enable the insurer to ascertain such amount and shall set forth such facts as will enable the insurer to ascertain the annuity contract, the annuitant and the payments sought to be avoided on the ground of fraud.

(2) The total exemption of benefits presently due and payable to any annuitant periodically or at stated times under all annuity contracts under which he or she is an annuitant, shall

not at any time exceed $350.00 per month for the length of time represented by such installments, and that such periodic payments in excess of $350.00 per month shall be subject to garnishee execution.

(3) If the total benefits presently due and payable to any annuitant under all annuity contracts under which he or she is an annuitant, shall at any time exceed payment at the rate of $350.00 per month, then the court may order such annuitant to pay to a judgment creditor or apply on the judgment, in installments, such portion of such excess benefits as to the court may appear just and proper, after due regard for the reasonable requirements of the judgment debtor and his or her family if dependent upon him or her, as well as any payments required to be made by the annuitant to other creditors under prior court orders.

(b) If the contract so provides, the benefits, rights, privileges or options accruing under such contract to a beneficiary or assignee shall not be transferable nor subject to commutation, and if the benefits are payable periodically or at stated times, the same exemptions and exceptions contained herein for the annuitant, shall apply with respect to such beneficiary or assignee.

Virginia

Life Insurance:

Beneficiary's interest in life insurance proceeds are exempt, provided the beneficiary is not the owner of the policy.

Group life insurance proceeds are exempt.

Virginia Code Annotated – Section 38.2-3122 – Proceeds of policies payable to others free of claims against insured.

The assignee or lawful beneficiary of an insurance policy shall be entitled to its proceeds against any claims of the creditors or representatives of the insured or the person effecting the policy, except in cases of transfer with intent to defraud creditors, subject to the following conditions:

1. The policy shall have been effected by a person on his own life or on another life, in favor of a person other than himself;

2. The assignee of the policy, or the payee, if the policy is otherwise made payable to another, shall not be the insured, nor the person effecting the policy, nor the executors or administrators;

3. The right to change the beneficiary may or may not have been reserved or permitted;

4. The policy may be payable to the person whose life is insured if the beneficiary or assignee predeceases the insured; and

5. Subject to the statute of limitations, the amount of any premiums for such policy paid with the intent to defraud creditors, or paid under such circumstances as to be void under § 55-81, with the interest thereon, shall be to the benefit of the creditors from the proceeds of the policy.

Virginia Code Annotated – Section 38.2-3339 – Exemption of group life insurance policies from legal process.

No group life insurance policy, nor its proceeds, shall be liable to attachment, garnishment, or other process, or to be seized, taken, appropriated, or applied by any legal or equitable process or operation of law, to pay any debt or liability of any person insured under the policy, or his beneficiary, or any other person who has a right under the policy, either before or after payment. If the proceeds of a group life insurance policy are not made payable to a named beneficiary, the proceeds shall not constitute a part of the insured person's estate for the payment of his debts.

Annuity Contract: No Specific Statute

Washington

Life Insurance:

Beneficiary's interest in life insurance proceeds are exempt, provided the beneficiary is not the owner of the policy.

Group life insurance proceeds are exempt.

Revised Code of Washington – Section 48.18.410 – Exemptions of proceeds – Life.

(1) The lawful beneficiary, assignee, or payee of a life insurance policy, other than an annuity, heretofore or hereafter effected by any person on his or her own life, or on the life of another, in favor of a person other than himself or herself, shall be entitled to the proceeds and avails of the policy against the creditors and representatives of the insured and of the person effecting the insurance, and such proceeds and avails shall also be exempt from all liability for any debt of such beneficiary, existing at the time the proceeds or avails are made available for his or her own use.

(2) The provisions of subsection (1) of this section shall apply

(a) whether or not the right to change the beneficiary is reserved or permitted in the policy; or

(b) whether or not the policy is made payable to the person whose life is insured or to his or her estate if the beneficiary, assignee or payee shall predecease such person; except, that this subsection shall not be construed so as to defeat any policy provision which provides for disposition of proceeds in the event the beneficiary shall predecease the insured.

(3) The exemptions provided by subsection (1) of this section, subject to the statute of limitations, shall not apply

(a) to any claim to or interest in such proceeds or avails by or on behalf of the insured, or the person so effecting the insurance, or their administrators or executors, in whatever capacity such claim is made or such interest is asserted; or

(b) to any claim to or interest in such proceeds or avails by or on behalf of any person to whom rights thereto have been transferred with intent to defraud creditors; but an insurer shall be liable to all such creditors only as to amounts aggregating not to exceed the amount of such proceeds or avails remaining in the insurer›s possession at the time the insurer receives at its home office written notice by or on behalf of such creditors, of claims to recover for such transfer, with specification of the amounts claimed; or

(c) to so much of such proceeds or avails as equals the amount of any premiums or portion thereof paid for the insurance with intent to defraud creditors, with interest thereon, and if prior to the payment of such proceeds or avails the insurer has received at its home office written notice by or on behalf of the creditor, of a claim to recover for premiums paid with intent to defraud creditors, with specification of the amount claimed.

(4) For the purposes of subsection (1) of this section a policy shall also be deemed to be payable to a person other than the insured if and to the extent that a facility-of-payment clause or similar clause in the policy permits the insurer to discharge its obligation after the death of the individual insured by paying the death benefits to a person as permitted by such clause.

(5) No person shall be compelled to exercise any rights, powers, options or privileges under any such policy.

Revised Code of Washington – Section 48.18.420 – Exemptions of proceeds – Group life.

(1) A policy of group life insurance or the proceeds thereof payable to the individual insured or to the beneficiary thereunder, shall not be liable, either before or after payment, to be applied to any legal or equitable process to pay any liability of any person having a right under the policy. The proceeds thereof, when not made payable to a named beneficiary or to a third person pursuant to a facility-of-payment clause, shall not constitute a part of the estate of the individual insured for the payment of his or her debts.

(2) This section shall not apply to group life insurance policies issued under RCW 48.24.040 (debtor groups) to the extent that such proceeds are applied to payment of the obligation for the purpose of which the insurance was so issued.

Annuity Contract:

Benefits up to $3,000 per month are exempt.

Revised Code of Washington – Section 48.18.430 – Exemptions of proceeds, commutation – Annuities.

(1) The benefits, rights, privileges, and options under any annuity contract that are due the annuitant who paid the consideration for the annuity contract are not subject to execution and the annuitant may not be compelled to exercise those rights, powers, or options, and creditors are not allowed to interfere with or terminate the contract, except:

(a) As to amounts paid for or as premium on an annuity with intent to defraud creditors, with interest thereon, and of which the creditor has given the insurer written notice at its home office prior to making the payments to the annuitant out of which the creditor seeks to recover. The notice must specify the amount claimed or the facts that will enable the insurer to determine the amount, and must set forth the facts that will enable the insurer to determine the insurance or annuity contract, the person insured or annuitant and the payments sought to be avoided on the basis of fraud.

(b) The total exemption of benefits presently due and payable to an annuitant periodically or at stated times under all annuity contracts may not at any time exceed three thousand dollars per month for the length of time represented by the installments, and a periodic payment in excess of three thousand dollars per month is subject to garnishee execution to the same extent as are wages and salaries.

(c) If the total benefits presently due and payable to an annuitant under all annuity contracts at any time exceeds payment at the rate of three thousand dollars per month, then the court may order the annuitant to pay to a judgment creditor or apply on the judgment, in installments, the portion of the excess benefits that the court determines to be just and proper, after due regard for the reasonable requirements of the judgment debtor and the judgment debtor's dependent family, as well as any payments required to be made by the annuitant to other creditors under prior court orders.

(2) The benefits, rights, privileges, or options accruing under an annuity contract to a beneficiary or assignee are not transferable or subject to commutation, and if the benefits are payable periodically or at stated times, the same exemptions and exceptions contained in this section for the annuitant apply to the beneficiary or assignee.

(3) An annuity contract within the meaning of this section is any obligation to pay certain sums at stated times, during life or lives, or for a specified term or terms, issued for a valuable consideration, regardless of whether or not the sums are payable to one or more persons, jointly or otherwise, but does not include payments under life insurance contracts at stated times during life or lives, or for a specified term or terms.

Washington, D.C.

Life Insurance:

Up to $200 per month is exempt if the beneficiary is providing the principal support of the family. Up to $60 per month is exempt if the beneficiary is not providing the principal support of the family.

District of Columbia Code Annotated – Section 15-503 – Exemptions of proceeds – Life.

(a) The earnings (other than wages, as defined in subchapter III of Chapter 5 of Title 16), insurance, annuities, or pension or retirement payments, not otherwise exempted, not to exceed $ 200 each month, of a person residing in the District of Columbia, or of a person who earns the major portions of his livelihood in the

District of Columbia, regardless of place of residence, who provides the principal support of a family, for two months next preceding the issuing of any writ or process against him, from any court or officer of and in the District, are exempt from attachment, levy, seizure, or sale upon the process, and may not be seized, levied on, taken, reached, or sold by process or proceedings of any court, judge, or other officer of and in the District. Where spouses or domestic partners are living together, the aggregate of the earnings, insurance, annuities, and pension or retirement payments of the spouses or domestic partners is the amount which shall be determinative of the exemption of either in cases arising ex contractu.

(b) The earnings (other than wages, as defined in subchapter III of Chapter 5 of Title 16), insurance, annuities, or pension or retirement payments, not otherwise exempt, not to exceed $ 60 each month for two months preceding the date of attachment of persons residing in the District of Columbia, or of persons who earn the major portions of their livelihood in the District of Columbia, regardless of place of residence, who do not provide for the support of a family, are entitled to like exemption from attachment, levy, seizure, or sale. All wearing apparel belonging to such persons, not exceeding $ 300 in value, and mechanic's tools not exceeding $ 200 in value, are also exempt.

Annuity Contract:

Payment under an annuity contract held within a 401(a) or 403(b) is exempt to the extent reasonably necessary to provide for support of debtor or a dependent of the debtor.

District of Columbia Code Annotated – Section 15-501 (a) (7)(E)– Exempt property of householder

(a) The following property of the head of a family or householder residing in the District of Columbia, or of a person who earns the major portion of his livelihood in the District of Columbia, being the head of a family or householder, regardless of his place of residence, is free and exempt from distraint, attachment, levy, or seizure and sale on execution or decree of any court in the District of Columbia:

(7) the debtor's right to receive:

(E) a payment under a stock bonus, pension, profit-sharing, annuity, or similar plan or contract on account of illness, disability, death, age, or length of service, to the extent reasonably necessary for the support of the debtor and any dependent of the debtor, unless:

(i) the plan or contract was established by or under the auspices of an insider that employed the debtor at the time the debtor›s rights under the plan or contract arose;

(ii) the payment is on account of age or length of service; and

(iii) the plan or contract does not qualify under section 401(a) or 403(b) of the Internal Revenue Code of 1986, approved October 22, 1986 (100 Stat. 2085; 26 U.S.C. § 1 et seq.) («1986 Code»);

West Virginia

Life Insurance:

Proceeds and avails of a life insurance policy are exempt.

West Virginia Code – Section 33-6-27 – Life insurance proceeds exempt from creditors.

(a) If a policy of insurance, whether heretofore or hereafter issued, is effected by any person on his own life or on another life, in favor of a person other than himself, or, except in cases of transfer with intent to defraud creditors, if a policy of life insurance is assigned or in any way made payable to any such person, the lawful beneficiary or assignee thereof, other than the insured or the person so effecting such insurance or executors or administrators of such insured or the person so effecting such insurance, shall be entitled to its proceeds and avails against the creditors and representatives of the insured and of the person effecting the same, whether or not the right to change the beneficiary is reserved or permitted, and whether or not the policy is made payable to the person whose life is insured if the beneficiary or assignee shall predecease such person.

(b) Subject to the statute of limitations, the amount of any premiums for such insurance paid in fraud of creditors, with interest thereon, shall inure to their benefit from the proceeds of the policy, but the insurer issuing the policy shall be discharged of all liability thereon by payment of the proceeds in accordance with its terms, unless before such payment the insurer received written notice by or in behalf of some creditor, with specification of the amount claimed, claiming to recover for certain premiums paid in fraud of creditors.

(c) For the purposes of paragraph (a), above, a policy shall also be deemed to be payable to a person other than the insured if and to the extent that a facility-of-payment clause or similar clause in the policy permits the insurer to discharge its obligations after the death of the individual insured by paying the death benefits to a person as permitted by such clause.

Annuity Contract:

Payment reasonably necessary for the support of the debtor and any dependent of the debtor under an annuity contract held within a 401(a), 403(a), 403(b), 408 or 409 is exempt.

West Virginia Code – Section 38- 10- 4(5)– Exemptions of property in bankruptcy proceedings.

(5) A payment under a stock bonus, pension, profit sharing, annuity or similar plan or contract on account of illness, disability, death, age or length of service, to the extent reasonably necessary for the support of the debtor and any dependent of the debtor, and funds on deposit in an individual retirement account (IRA), including a simplified employee pension (SEP) regardless of the amount of funds, unless:

> (A) The plan or contract was established by or under the auspices of an insider that employed the debtor at the time the debtor's rights under the plan or contract arose;

(B) The payment is on account of age or length of service;

(C) The plan or contract does not qualify under Section 401(a), 403(a), 403(b), 408 or 409 of the Internal Revenue Code of 1986; and

(D) With respect to an individual retirement account, including a simplified employee pension, the amount is subject to the excise tax on excess contributions under Section 4973 and/or Section 4979 of the Internal Revenue Code of 1986, or any successor provisions, regardless of whether the tax is paid.

Wisconsin

Life Insurance and Annuity Contract:

Any unmatured life insurance or annuity contract is exempt up to $150,000 in any accrued dividends, interest, or loan value to the debtor or debtor's dependent.

The exemption is limited to $4,000 if the life insurance or annuity contract was issued less than 24 months of the applicable date.

If the life insurance policy or annuity contract was issued at least 24 months but funded in less than 24 months the exemption is limited to $4,000.

Wisconsin Statutes – Section 815.18(3)(f)(2) and (3) – Property exempt from executions – Life insurance and annuities.

(f) Life insurance and annuities.

1. In this paragraph, "applicable date" means the earlier of the following:

The date on which the exemption is claimed.

b. The date, if any, that the cause of action was filed that resulted in the judgment with respect to which the execution order was issued.

2. Except as provided in subd. 3. and par. (j), any unmatured life insurance or annuity contract owned by the debtor and insuring the debtor, the debtor's dependent, or an individual of whom the debtor is a dependent, other than a credit life insurance contract, and the debtor's aggregate interest, not to exceed $150,000 in value, in any accrued dividends, interest, or loan value of all unmatured life insurance or annuity contracts owned by the debtor and insuring the debtor, the debtor's dependent, or an individual of whom the debtor is a dependent.

3.

a. If the life insurance or annuity contract was issued less than 24 months before the applicable date, the exemption under this paragraph may not exceed $4,000.

If the life insurance or annuity contract was issued at least 24 months but funded less than 24 months before the applicable date, the exemption under this paragraph is limited to the value of the contract the day before the first funding that occurred less than 24 months before the applicable date and the lesser of either the difference between the value of the contract the day before the first funding that occurred less than 24 months before the applicable date and the value of the contract on the applicable date or $4,000.

Wyoming

Life Insurance:

Life insurance proceeds are exempt.

Group life insurance proceeds and avails are exempt.

Wyoming Statutes Annotated – Section 26-15-129 – Exemption of proceeds; life insurance.

(a) If a policy of insurance is executed by any person on his own life or on another life, in favor of a person other than himself, or except in cases of transfer with intent to defraud creditors, if a policy of life insurance is assigned or in any way made payable to that person, the lawful beneficiary or assignee thereof, other than the insured or the person executing insurance or executors or administrators of the insured or the person executing the insurance, are entitled to its proceeds, including death benefits, cash surrender and loan values, premiums waived and dividends, whether used in reduction of premiums or otherwise, excepting only where the debtor, subsequent to issuance of the policy, has actually elected to receive the dividends in cash, against the creditors and representatives of the insured and of the person executing the policy, and are not liable to be applied by any legal or equitable process to pay any debt or liability of the insured individual or his beneficiary or of any other person having a right under the policy, whether or not:

(i) The right to change the beneficiary is reserved or permitted; and

(ii) The policy is made payable to the person whose life is insured if the beneficiary or assignee predeceases that person, and the proceeds are exempt from all liability for any debt of the beneficiary existing at the time the policy is made available for his use.

(b) However, subject to the statute of limitations, the amount of any premiums paid for insurance with intent to defraud creditors, with interest thereon, shall inure to their benefit from the policy proceeds; but the insurer issuing the policy is discharged of all liability thereon by payment of its proceeds in accordance with its terms, unless before payment the insurer receives written notice at its home office, by or in behalf of a creditor of:

(i) A claim to recover for transfer made or premiums paid with intent to defraud creditors;

(ii) The amount claimed along with facts as will assist the insurer to ascertain the particular policy.

(c) For the purposes of subsections (a) and (b) of this section, a policy is payable to a person other than the insured if and to the extent that a facility-of-payment clause or similar clause in the policy permits the insurer to discharge its obligation after the death of the individual insured by paying the death benefits to a person as permitted by the clause.

Wyoming Statutes Annotated – Section 26-15-129 – Exemption of proceeds; group insurance.

(a) A policy of group life insurance or group disability insurance or the proceeds thereof, including death benefits, cash surrender and loan values, premiums waived and dividends, whether used in reduction of premiums or otherwise, excepting only where the debtor, subsequent to issuance of the policy, has actually elected to receive the dividends in cash, payable to the individual insured or to the named beneficiary are not liable to be applied by any legal or equitable process to pay any debt or liability of the insured individual or his beneficiary or of any other person having a right under the policy. The proceeds, when not made payable to a named beneficiary, or to a third person pursuant to a facility-of-payment clause, do not constitute a part of the insured individual's estate for the payment of his debts.

(b) This section does not apply to group insurance issued pursuant to this code to a creditor covering his debtors, to the extent that the proceeds are applied to payment of the obligation for the purpose of which the insurance is issued.

Annuity Contract:

Benefits up to $350 per month are exempt.

Wyoming Statutes Annotated – Section 26-15-129 – Exemption of proceeds; annuity contracts; assignability of rights.

(a) The benefits, rights, privileges and options which under any annuity contract issued are due or prospectively due the annuitant, are not subject to execution nor is the annuitant compelled to exercise any such rights, powers or options. Creditors are not allowed to interfere with or terminate the contract, except:

(i) As to amounts paid for or as premium on the annuity with intent to defraud creditors, with interest thereon, and of which the creditor gives the insurer written notice at its home office prior to the making of the payment to the annuitant out of which the creditor seeks to recover, which notice shall specify:

(A) The amount claimed or facts to enable the ascertainment of the amount; and

(B) Facts to enable the insurer to ascertain the annuity contract, the annuitant and the payment sought to be avoided on the ground of fraud.

(ii) The total exemption of benefits presently due and payable to any annuitant periodically or at stated times under all annuity contracts under which he is an annuitant shall not at any time exceed three hundred fifty dollars ($350.00) per month for the length of time represented by the installments, and any periodic payments in excess of three hundred fifty dollars ($350.00) per month are subject to garnishee execution to the same extent as are wages and salaries;

(iii) If the total benefits presently due and payable to any annuitant under any annuity contracts at any time exceed three hundred fifty dollars ($350.00) per month, the court may order the annuitant to pay to a judgment creditor or apply on the judgment, in installments, that portion of the excess benefits as to the court appear just and proper, after regard for the reasonable requirements of the judgment debtor and his family, if dependent upon him, as well as any payments required to be made by the annuitant to other creditors under prior court order.

(b) If the contract provides, the benefits, rights, privileges or options accruing under that contract to a beneficiary or assignee are not transferable nor subject to commutation, and if the benefits are payable periodically or at stated times, the same exemptions and exceptions contained in this section for the annuitant, apply to the beneficiary or assignee.

Made in the USA
Middletown, DE
15 February 2016